D0111794

WHEN HISTORY ENTERS THE HOUSE:
ESSAYS FROM CENTRAL EUROPE

WHEN HISTORY ENTERS THE HOUSE:
ESSAYS FROM CENTRAL EUROPE

Michael Blumenthal

Pleasure Boat Studio

Cover Photograph: Susan Kaufman
Author Photograph: Isabelle Leconte
Design and Composition: Shannon Gentry

PUBLISHED BY PLEASURE BOAT STUDIO
802 EAST SIXTH
PORT ANGELES, WA 98362
U.S.A.

Tel-Fax: 360-452-8686
E-mail: pbstudio@pbstudio.com
URL: http://www.pbstudio.com

ISBN 0-9651413-2-2
LCCN 97-69066

Printed in the United States of America by Thomson-Shore

The Euroslavic Garamond fonts used to print this work
are available from Linguist's Software, Inc.,
P.O. Box 580, Edmonds, WA 98020-0580 USA Tel. 206-775-1130

FIRST PRINTING

ACKNOWLEDGMENTS

The essays and poems in this collection previously appeared—occasionally under a different title or in a slightly different form—in the following magazines, periodicals and newspapers:

BUDAPEST WEEK
When the Ghosts Have Bodies • A. A.: The Extraterritorial • Election Postscript
The Giant Who Goes Part-Way with Me • Elegy for the Lángos
Looking for "Árpi Bácsi" • Hello to All That • Waiting for Bread in Hegymagas
Real Family Values • Famous for Sixteen Seconds

THE BUDAPEST SUN
In Praise of Anarchy • And Their Flags Are Still There • George Konrád: An
Appreciation • So Many Borders, So Little Interest
This Private(ized) Life • Here's to the Happy Hungarians!
For Whom the Bell Tolls • When Freedom's Just Another Word
When History Enters the House • Tale of Two Schools
Primer for Hungarian Journalists • The (Un)Wisdom of (In)Security
Temple of Unanswered Prayers • Weinstock Among the Living
In Search of a Central European Metaphor: The Hanger
Report from the Home Front • Revenge of the Telephone • Visit to Majdanek

DOUBLETAKE
What I Loveth Well, Remains American

ESSAYS IN AMERICAN STUDIES
"Je change, donc je suis ... " (Eötvös Loránd University)

THE HARVARD REVIEW
In Praise of Battered Cities

THE HUNGARIAN QUARTERLY
The Allure of Exile
On the Loneliness of Hungarians

MAGYAR NARANC
Triumph of the Tawdry: O. J. Simpson

THE PARIS REVIEW
A Conversation with George Konrád

PRAIRIE SCHOONER
Visit to Majdanek
Temple of Unanswered Prayers
Lukács Fürdű: December 31, 1995

TIME MAGAZINE
Germany: The Sins of the Fathers

FOR MY FRIENDS, THE HUNGARIANS
&
FOR ISABELLE AND NOAH,
WHO HELPED MAKE IT POSSIBLE

PREFACE

Exile—whether it be forced or self-imposed, political or cultural, temporary or permanent—creates in the one exiled a kind of double vision: One looks at what remains, and will always remain (inescapably, I think), one's own country, perhaps for the first time, from afar; one looks at one's adopted country, though physically present in it, through a stranger's eyes. Hopefully, in doing so, one learns something about, and—if one is blessed with the kind of *echt*-romantic luck rarely, if ever, found in literature *or* in life—falls in love with, both. And, in the process, like it or not, one invariably learns something about oneself.

I came to Hungary, during that still-metamorphosing summer of 1992, more or less by accident: My wife and I wanted to get out of a certain infuriatingly contradictory (but, to me, still lovable) country—America—for a while, and, as fate would have it, met a couple of very likable Hungarians in Cambridge who informed us there were openings for Fulbrighters to Hungary. Five or so months later, there we were, living along a dirt road beside the railroad tracks in a part of Budapest (the 14th District, or Zugló) that several of our more cosmopolitan Hungarian friends quickly dubbed "Siberia."

We ourselves became more and more "cosmopolitan" as our four years in Budapest unfolded (and the Zugló, during that same period, became more and more "fashionable"), and as my own love affair with Budapest and with all things Hungarian developed, edged closer and closer to the Danube and the more "uppity" Buda side until, finally, we sat, almost literally, upon its shores. That movement, too, signaled a deeper and deeper involvement in, and love for, things Hungarian, for—as Joseph Brodsky has pointed out in his remarkable essay, "The Condition We Call Exile"—it is impossible to continue living in a foreign place for very long while resisting its language and culture and, at the same time, continuing to long for one's original home.

Blessedly for this writer, Hungary—its rich history and complicated culture; its lyrical albeit sometimes impenetrable language; its sensuous, melancholic and beautiful people; its ravishingly beautiful capital and subtly picturesque towns and villages—proved an almost impossible place to resist, reminding me that one of the blessed propinquities that allows a place of exile to become, even temporarily, one's home is the strange resonance of spirit and disposition one sometimes finds—

with a foreign place—the kind of resonance, to mention only a few of my betters, Paul Bowles no doubt felt with Tangiers, Gertrude Stein and James Baldwin with Paris, Isaak Dinesen with Kenya...and, yes, Joseph Brodsky with America.

But, appealing though a period of exile may be, with its removal from the hype, intimacies, networks and lack of anonymity one must, inevitably, endure in one's own country, one also longs, ultimately, not for the *ersatz* satisfactions of being a big fish in a small pond, but for what Wallace Stevens appropriately called "a gallery of one's own." There are few things sadder, I think, in the literary or personal life of a writer than having to resort to the grim, and illusory, literary satisfactions of having readers and "followers" merely among a community of those who have (all too often for reasons of overly meager gifts) fled from the only community that, for a writer, ultimately counts: his or her own countrymen, the speakers and purveyors of his or her own language.

The following essays were almost all written in Budapest between September of 1992 and May of 1996. As many of them were journalistic pieces written at a particular historical and political moment, I have included, after each, the date of its composition, so as to give the reader a sense of where it fits within the landscape of this rapidly evolving period in Central European—and, in particular, Hungarian—history. Though some of these essays deal with matters, so to speak, "purely American," I have chosen to include them, given my fundamental agreement with something James Baldwin wrote some forty years ago in an essay entitled, "A Question of Identity":

> From the vantage point of Europe, he [the American] discovers his own country. And this is a discovery which not only brings to an end the alienation of the American from himself, but which also makes clear to him, for the first time, the extent of his involvement in the life of Europe.

Though it is that once "other" Europe I am mostly writing about, and from, the principle, I believe, is still the same. I am the second generation offspring of European immigrants, married to a European woman, madly in love with a European mistress (Budapest), father to a "European"-speaking (French, Hungarian...and now, Hebrew) child. Like it or not (and I *do*), Europe—much to my amazement,

Central/Eastern Europe in particular—has become part of me: *Ich auch bin ein Budapestian.*

Which is not to say that the essays which follow are without their emotional vacillations and ambivalences, what Faulkner would have called their "divided heart." Such mixed feelings come not only with the condition of living in general, but also with that of exile in particular; for the latter is, by definition, a condition of "betweenness," of living between the country one has left, inalterably one's own, and the country one has fallen in love with, which can never entirely be. A condition—how else can I say it?—of simultaneously living within both a passionate yet somehow impossible affair and a deeply rooted though somehow uninspiring marriage. "I must leave!" the impassioned adulterer cries out. "I must stay!" replies the faithfully grounded spouse. And so, too, with nations.

I am grateful to numerous Hungarian friends—most notably Eszter Füzéki, Benedek and Marci Várkonyi and Andrea Ritter, László Kúnos and Gabriella Fekete, Júlia Debreczeni and Miklós Törkenczy, George Konrád and Judit Lakner, Huba Bruckner and the entire Hungarian Fulbright staff, Ádám Nádasdy, Tibor Frank, András Kepes and Lili Messmer, András Bor and Nóra Kováts, Péter Kántor, Miklós Vajda, László Földényi, Zoltán Kövecses, and (though she can't read this) Vera-néni—without whose friendship, generosity and intelligence I could not possibly have felt, during those four wonderful years, as "Hungarian" as I did. Nor am I able to name here the countless casual contacts of everyday life—the locker room attendants at the Lukács Fürdő, the ticket sellers at the puppet theatre, the soulful faces at the *cukrászda* (pastry shop) and *zöldség-gyümölcs* (fruit and vegetable) stands, the *nénis* (aunts) and *bácsis* (uncles)—who made of virtually every moment I spent in the for-me-unlikely nation of Hungary one I will treasure all my sentient life…and perhaps thereafter.

I also want to thank both the U. S. Fulbright Commission and the Hungarian-American Fulbright Commission in Budapest, and the American Studies Department at Eötvös Loránd University for a three-year Senior Fulbright Lectureship, without the support of which these essays could not have been written.

Finally, my gratitude, and love to Jack Estes and Shannon Gentry—friends, godparents, publishers, editors, and fellow travelers—joined to my family and myself, in one of those wonderful synchronicities that compose a life, by Hungary as well.

WE THOUGHT WE WERE HAVING LUNCH. LATER
WE REALIZED IT WAS 'HISTORY.'

SÁNDOR MÁRAI,
LAND! LAND!

CONTENTS

PROLOGUE

The Hustle

The walls go up. The walls go down.
Everyone's getting ready to do The Hustle.

Money talks. Everyone walks
And slowly gets ready to do The Hustle.

No more poets in the dark cafés.
They're all too busy learning The Hustle.

You're rich. You're poor. You're learning to play
At that old nasty dance known as The Hustle.

Benetton. Reebok. Calvin Klein on the way.
The whole world is laughing and doing The Hustle.

You're tired? You're nervous? You used to be gay?
Just relax. And be happy you're doing The Hustle.

It was good for America. It could be for you.
So stop *kvetching* already. And let's do The Hustle.

PART I

THE SINS OF THE FATHERS

GERMANY:
THE SINS OF THE FATHERS

> They surrounded me. One tried to touch
> my hair. When I turned toward him he
> quickly withdrew his hand. They exchanged
> remarks about me. Although I could not
> understand very much I heard the word
> "Gypsy" many times.
>
> JERZY KOSINSKI
> *THE PAINTED BIRD* (1965)

The Germans (along with the Hungarians and others), are at it again ("it" being the killing, hounding, and epithet-hurling at those who are racially "other"), and—as the son of German-Jewish refugees who escaped, by the skin of their teeth and the vicissitudes of luck, the ravages of the Nazi Holocaust—it is easy (a bit *too* easy, I suspect) to feel an almost visceral dislike for the Germans, to be willing, in matters moral, never to give them the benefit of the doubt. After all, it was not merely a handful, but *millions*, of Germans who at least part-knowingly acquiesced in what still seems the unspeakable: the organized, systematic gassing and torture of six million innocent Jews, Gypsies, and others, an act that has left scars on both the Germans and their victims, scars which it may take all remaining human history to heal, and memories which ought *never* be erased.

All intellectualizations as to Hannah Arendt's now-famous "banality of evil" theory notwithstanding, the Germans, either justly or unjustly, are held to a higher burden of proof when moral and racial matters, such as the current treatment and status of Germany's 1.4 million refugees, many of them Gypsies, are at stake. And though the sins of the fathers are, rightly or wrongly, visited upon the sons, it is also a fact that the *victimization* of the fathers may, at times, lead to the sins of the sons. So that in judging the present emotion-filled crisis of the refugee presence in Germany, a person may need all the more to strive for a certain even-handedness and objectivity in his or her judgment, lest yet another tragic lesson of history—namely, that all ethnic and religious hatreds and tragedies perpetuate and reinforce one another—be reenacted in our time.

Whether or not the "new" generation of Germans—those who by the mere fact of their post-War birth cannot in any way be held responsible for the sins (whether of omission or commission) of their ancestors—deserve to be held to a different standard than the rest of us is, no doubt, a question best answered by moral philosophers and theologians. For myself, an affirmative answer would merely, once again, invoke the kind of racial double-standard that has, time and again, led to tragedy in the first place. For it is morally simplistic to use the irreparability of the German crimes of the Nazi era as a justification for dismissing whatever efforts individual Germans may be making at reparation and repentance today. (How much morally less significant, we might ask, were the sins of slavery, and how adequate have our own efforts to "repair" them been?) There is a certain easy solace, I fear, in labeling one crime (however compelling the label) as history's "worst," one people as history's most egregious villains. It allows the rest of us, by implication, to be subjected to a lower standard of morality, to enjoy an easier sleep.

It is useful, I think, to cast a certain cold eye on contemporary Germany's record *vis a vis* Gypsies and others before we judge it too harshly, to understand where, in fact, Germany and most contemporary Germans (for example, the more than 300,000 who recently marched *against* racism in Berlin) stand before we pronounce our easy and self-righteous *j'accuse*. We might remember, for example, that the German constitution today includes the most liberal and generous policy toward asylum-seekers anywhere in the world (and also to remind the Germans that one motive behind that policy, along with generosity of spirit, was to provide a source of cheap labor for jobs most Germans didn't want—and could at the time afford to pass up). That policy guarantees to anyone who merely utters the word *"asyl"* or "asylum" on German soil—expected to be some 450,000 by the end of this year alone—the right to be sheltered and fed during the months, and sometimes years, while their case is considered. We might consider that in *any* nation in which (as is presently the case in what was formerly East Germany) nearly 40% of the labor force suffers from some sort of "voluntary" or involuntary unemployment, the presence of so many job-seeking and unemployed refugees, supported at government expense, would be the target of economic unrest and accumulated rage. We should remember that, for every enraged, anarchic, possibly pro-Fascist German throwing rocks and eggs and tomatoes at President von Weizsäcker the other week, there were thousands more standing *up* (rather than *by,* as they did during the Nazi era) to proclaim their shame at their country's past, and their repugnance for this particular aspect of its present.

We should look at all this before—in our haste to condemn the Germans and relieve ourselves of our own moral burdens—the sins of the fathers now become, in the utmost of ironies, the sins of someone else's sons. And we should remember that freedom, as well as democracy, is best served when human beings are treated not as members of a group but as individuals—and not only those who deserve to be punished, but also those who deserve to be forgiven.

OCTOBER 1992

WHEN THE GHOSTS HAVE BODIES

We are all, no doubt, haunted by the ghosts of our backgrounds and upbringings, spending much of our later life trying to correct their distortions and misperceptions. I, for one, was raised by German-Jewish refugees who fled to New York from Nazi Germany in 1938 in the no-doubt-understandable, but to me wrong-minded, belief that an anti-Semite lurked behind every bush; that all non-Jews, somewhere deep down, harbored such sentiments; that the world was a fundamentally hostile place in which no Jew could ever feel entirely safe and secure.

From a very young age—young enough, I now realize, not to fully understand how or why the bigotry and hatred my parents had been the victims of could lead them also to become bigoted and hateful—I detested their racial hatreds, much as I detested the bigotry and hate that had brought them to what is now my country. I hated their racist attitudes toward Blacks, Puerto Ricans, Christians in general (those terrible "*goyim*"), and—perhaps worst of all—toward those Eastern European Jews who, having not ever been as "German" as they were, were, ergo, even more Jewish. Amid the conundrum of these many hatreds and self-hatreds, these paranoia and suspicions, I vowed to myself from a very young age that *I*, at least, would not live in such a world—that, for me, all of mankind would be innocent until proven guilty, every individual presumed to be without racism or bigotry until I had good reason to believe otherwise.

This belief has, in fact, served me well in my adult life, and it is one I intend to stand by until my dying day. Indeed, I have found most of the people I have come in contact with—Blacks, Christians, Jews, Moslems, Germans, Hungarians, Hispanics, etc.—to be people of good will and tolerance, eager to see others as individuals rather than representatives of racial, religious, or social castes. When I turned toward the blackboard of a high school German class I was teaching in upstate New York back in 1969 and found a chalky swastika emblazoned there, it was not my bleak view of human nature that was confirmed, but rather my optimistic view of human possibilities that was somewhat tarnished.

Experience, notwithstanding such isolated instances, has continued to teach me that human nature, though flawed, is fundamentally (except, of course, under conditions of the severest stress) decent, generous, open-minded. I truly believe—in America, in France (where my wife is from), in Germany, and now in Hungary—that I have encountered few genuine anti-Semites in my life. And it is a label which I will always refuse to use carelessly or exploitively or in search of an undeserved self-pity. For what my parents' and their generation's experiences have truly taught me is the danger of *all* such labels, the injustice of *all* such hatreds.

So that—coming here to Hungary some two months ago—it was with a certain self-cautionary whisper into my own ear that I began to hear the many rumors and innuendoes concerning Hungarian anti-Semitism, and I had to remind myself once again of my own evidentiary rules. Indeed, my experience thus far only confirms my general principles: I have, to my knowledge, neither met an anti-Semite of any sort here in Budapest, nor been in any way mistreated or ignored because of my own Jewishness.

Nonetheless, when I begin to see one of Hungary's most generous and democratically minded philanthropists, George Soros, attacked by ruling party vice-president and member of Parliament István Csurka for being more responsive to "official policy in Jerusalem" than to his country's own needs; when I read the article by MDF member of Parliament Gyula Zacsek stating, "I do not understand what it means to be a 'Hungarian Jew' any more than I would understand what it would mean if someone claimed to be a Hungarian-German or a Hungarian-Vietnamese or a German-Spaniard," a certain worrisome echo of my parents'

10

despised worldview begins to manifest itself in me: I begin, sadly, to wonder if they may have been right.

The fact is that, though I may wonder, I know: They were *not* right, and my refusal to abide by their enemy-ridden view of the world remains unchanged. I know too much of the many Germans and other Europeans who risked their lives to *help* endangered Jews during the life-threatening years of the Holocaust; I know too much (already) of the tens of thousands of Hungarians (as manifested in the pro-democracy march to Parliament several weeks ago) who despise Csurka's and Zacsek's views, and everything they stand for; I know too many committed and courageously democratic and egalitarian-minded individuals of all races and persuasions in my own country to believe in such a hate- and bigotry-dominated world.

But one thing, now more than ever, has also become clear to me in my still-brief time here in Hungary: Namely, that those of us who despise and detest and are committed with all our flesh and spirit to the defeat of such anti-human sentiments must continue, at all costs and without hesitation, to speak out. And that about at least one thing even my often-bigoted and hateful (and themselves victimized) parents may have been right: Even paranoids have enemies; even a certain paranoia may, sadly, sometimes be justified, if only to protect us from the even worse darkness that may still lie ahead.

OCTOBER 1992

VISIT TO MAJDANEK

Lublin, Poland. It is—how else can I say it?—a beautiful day in the south of Poland. The air is crisp and clean; crows alight and rise up from the grass-covered, once torture-ridden, fields. As I emerge from the "new" crematorium—whose ovens, I am told by a tactfully brief placard inside, could produce a "yield" (reminding me of Hannah Arendt's starkly unsentimental description of Auschwitz as a "corpse factory") of over one thousand bodies daily—a white-and-brown fox hastily beats a retreat into a hole just below one of the SS guards' watchtowers. In the not-far-off distance, the new and old buildings of Lublin, the eerily evocative smokestacks, can be seen, and the morbid thought crosses my mind that—were this another place, were this another life—this might be a good place, a good day, for a picnic...or maybe it still is.

On the single day of November 3, 1943—exactly fifty-one years from the day I am writing this—some 18,400 Jews were shot and dumped into the execution ditches close to the crematorium at Majdanek, just outside of Lublin. In all, between 1941 and its liberation in the autumn of 1944, through a combination of insufferable living conditions and direct executions, some 360,000 persons—many, but not all, of them Jews—lost their lives here. It is a number which encompasses many times all those I have ever known, much less loved, a number so staggering in terms of actual human lives, of unlived human potential, that only the 800,000 pairs of victims' shoes gathered in wire bins at Majdanek—men's shoes, women's shoes, children's like my own son's shoes—are capable, somehow, of concretizing it, of—in the words of Israeli writer and Holocaust survivor, Aharon Appelfeld—"giving the tortured person back his human form."

I had never before been to a concentration camp, a visit to which has become one of my generation's "rites of passage" into the dark underbelly of 20th-century Jewish history. Though I am told by the brochure that "the guides of the Polish Tourist Country-Lovers' Association (PTTK)"—a name I cannot help but wince at while reading—"are also qualified to take tourists round the Museum," it seems best to do this alone…alone, that is, with the ghosts of the past.

The visitor to a place such as Majdanek always asks himself—*must*, I suspect, ask himself—before going, the inevitable questions: *Why go? Why hunt down such evil, go actively in search of it—I who have "escaped," remained, superficially, untouched?* But the answers are also rather obvious—so obvious, perhaps, as to obviate the questions. We are not, any of us, "untouched." We have not, any of us, "escaped." And because it is our destiny in this life to attempt to visit those regions of beauty and love which defy speech—we must also contemplate that other unspeakable reality of our lives: absolute evil. *Hier,* as a Nazi guard at Auschwitz once told the Italian-Jewish writer Primo Levi, *ist kein warum* ("Here there is no why, nothing that needs be explained").

"Go there," the Hungarian writer George Konrád told me in 1993 when I mentioned never having been to a camp. "Go there. I would suggest it to you, and to everyone," he said. "I was not there until '82, and I said 'Why should I go there, I can imagine it?' However, it's good to go there, to touch those walls and to look at those shoes and to look at the hill of hair which is now completely gray, because it was once maybe black and blonde and brown, all kinds of hair. But it became gray, the whole stuff. It's good to be there. And to touch somehow the extremes, to touch the walls of the executions."

To touch the walls of the executions. One likes to think of the concentration camps as, somehow, located "out of sight" (ergo, potentially out of mind), in venues remote, secreted, exempt from the daily gazes and contemplations of the local citizenry. Therefore, from the shocking moment when one first comes upon Majdanek, it jars the senses, shatters one's moral and moralizing boundaries. Located so close to the center of Lublin (once the center of a richly varied and influential Jewish community numbering some 40,000) that, to put it crudely, a profit-minded entrepreneur might well choose the site for a shopping mall or drive-in, the physical fact of Majdanek itself starkly belies the myth of the innocent and unknowing bystander.

And so—even before we step onto its fields of torture and degradation, even before we set foot into its crematoria and barracks—Majdanek confronts us with a primary, only slightly less unspeakable, reality: They *knew,* and, being here, we now *know* that they knew, and thus we are forced, not merely to accuse, but to ask ourselves: "What if *we* knew? What is it, at this very moment, that *we* know and remain passive in the face of, preferring not to see, to know, to act? One is forced, in other words, to reconsider one's use of adjectives: Was it purely *Nazi* evil that occurred at Majdanek? Or just *goyishe* evil? Or—that ugliest of possibilities, already considered in great detail and eloquence by Hannah Arendt—merely *human* evil?

This being the information age, here, too, information abounds. And, like all "information," it is easily confused and confusing, threatening to obscure real feelings with mere facts. "The prisoners of Majdanek came from 29 states all over the world (according to the world political map of 1938)," says one brochure. "Poles were most numerous, constituting nearly 40% of the total number. Jews constituted 30%." The official museum brochure explains, "In the years 1941-1944, some 500,000 inmates of 54 nationalities passed through Majdanek." And my own guidebook puts it this way: "It's hard to take in the brutal fact that over 200,000 people of more than twenty nations were murdered here, a significant number of them Jews." But what's in a number, when one considers an evil of such magnitude? A fact by any other name is equally harsh.

Hands in my pockets, looking up, down, around, I walk past the mausoleum, where the ashes of prisoners executed at Majdanek, once used as fertilizer, mingle with the earth. Even here, I can't help notice half-guiltily how all the abstract pieties of the human mind—or, at least, of *my* human mind—distanced as they are from the brutal specificities of such events, how they do not resist the obscuring imperatives of desire and pleasure: The young Polish girl standing staring out at the Mausoleum before me, I still notice, is exceptionally pretty.

I continue past the mass execution ditches, now overgrown with grass; past the overseers' barracks and the barracks that housed several of the camp's gas chambers. I walk past the horrifically named "Field of Roses," the selection square in front of the bathhouses, within sight of which—

as if to suggest a universe as indifferent to evil as it is resilient with beauty—roses still grow. I enter the bath houses and gas chambers of the old crematorium, so silent and eerily clean that hardly the ghosts of the dead seem able to disturb them, and I open the door of the small cell from which certain SS officers would introduce pellets of Cyclone-B gas through holes in the ceiling and then, through a small, grated window opening out into the chamber itself, watch their prisoners die. I remember, as I close the door, Irving Howe's well-known formulation of disequivalence: "In classical tragedy man was defeated; in the Holocaust he was destroyed. "

There is so much to see here—so many photos and facts, so many shoes and rooms, so many hectares of land, so many images of torture and degradation and death. But, in the end, as Peter Davies wrote of Auschwitz, it is "all these things, cumulatively crushing you, a seeping of evil from every wall and corner of the place, from every brick and block, until you reach your limit and it overwhelms you." In the end, you are simply left to walk out into the fields and gaze at the nearby hills of Lublin, at the grasses and roses and smokestacks of this world. You are left to praise whatever there may be left to praise. You are left to contemplate yourself and your kind.

NOVEMBER 1994

TEMPLE OF UNANSWERED PRAYERS

Kőszeg, Hungary. The silence surrounding it—interrupted only by the occasional chirping of a sparrow or the cawing of a crow from atop one of its forsaken towers—is at least equally heart-rending as the sounds of prayers that once filled it. For it, and ruins like it all over Eastern Europe—in their utter dilapidation and abandonment, their surrounding mini-jungle of overgrown weeds, vines and hedges—are perhaps more poignant, and more melancholy, reminders of the fate of East European Jewry than even the gas chambers of the concentration camps, the burial pits and the skeletal, filigreed *"Arbeit Macht Frei"* that hangs over the gates of Auschwitz.

As you walk through the neo-Gothic Heroes' Gate and into the historic Belváres (Inner City) district of the quaint little town of Kőszeg in Western Transdanubia—sometimes referred to, I cannot help but observe ironically, as the nation's 'jewelry box'—you must, in fact, make a certain effort to locate the crumbling, circular brick towers at Várkör 34 which once served one of the oldest Jewish communities in Hungary. You must perhaps, as I did, first knock on the door of Ernő Kolnhofer at Várkör 38 and ask to be allowed into his courtyard and, then, graciously enough, onto his second-floor patio in order to stand for

The abandoned Jewish synagogue at Kőszeg.

a moment and survey what remains of the house of worship that—at the height of Kőszeg's Jewish community around 1941 (not long before Kőszeg became the headquarters of the Hungarian Arrow Cross)— served some one hundred individuals, a building recently purchased by a local former Communist Party secretary named Gusztáv Krug, whose original plan was to turn it into a beer hall (*söröző*).

You must remain here, perhaps, for many moments and listen to the long silence of unanswered prayers, then gaze for a long time at the scarred and hardly recognizable twin tablets containing the Ten Commandments that are the only exterior evidence of the building's once-sacred origins, in order to appreciate the fact that it is not merely yet another "ordinary" ruined building you are staring at, but an edifice within whose now-crumbling walls dozens of the soon-to-be-slaughtered millions turned their eyes toward a seemingly deaf and unsympathetic God and prayed, unsuccessfully, for their and their loved ones' salvation.

For Kőszeg, not unlike many smaller and larger towns and villages throughout Hungary, is haunted by the sounds and sights, by the resonant echoes, of Jewish history. Along with nearby Sopron, it was one of the two cities in Western Transdanubia's Vas County where Jews lived during the Middle Ages. As early as 1420—at the time when they were also forced to leave lower Austria and Vienna—Kőszeg's Jews were first forced to flee, not returning again until approximately 1509, only to be evicted once more by the Habsburg emperor in 1565, and to return once more during the final years of the 18th Century. According to a 1788 census, there were only two Jewish families residing in Kőszeg at the time, a number which grew to approximately fourteen adults by 1807.

The neo-Gothic synagogue itself, occupying an interior space of 30.6-x-12.8 meters, was built between 1858 and 1859 with donations from local Jewish merchant Fülöp Schey , later elevated to the status of Count by the Austrian Habsburgs. Inside, its cupola still displays a rich, Baroque-style painting bearing the German words, *"in Ehre Gottes gebaut von Philip Schey von Koromla"* ("built in praise of God by Philip Schey von Koromla"). The two crumbling outbuildings—which now resemble, more than anything, tombstones in an abandoned cemetery—once housed, to the synagogue's right, a *mikva*, or ritual bath, and, to the left, a Hebrew school classroom and teacher's apartment. Now, as with most of Hungary's well-over one hundred mostly abandoned synagogues, they are home only to insects and rats...and to the persistence of memory.

WHEN HISTORY ENTERS THE HOUSE

"I myself am Catholic," says Ernő Kolnhofer, a frog-eyed, highly sympathetic man approximately my own age whose disarrayed house and thinly veiled comments suggest he is in the midst of a marital upheaval, "but I think it is disgraceful that anyone would think of turning such a house of worship into a beer hall." Others, led by Hungary's surviving Jewish community and its Historic Preservation Law, apparently shared Kolnhofer's feelings, for it seems that public sentiment ultimately prevailed over Krug's entrepreneurial vision, though the building's actual future remains uncertain. According to Kolnhofer, architects have estimated that it would cost approximately five million forints (roughly $400,000 U.S.) to restore the synagogue to its original state. Several years ago an American teacher, hoping to raise the money, staged a series of concerts and other fund-raising events in Kőszeg, but he fell far short of the mark. And the issue—namely, of finding both the collective will and the funds with which to restore and preserve synagogues in towns and villages whose Jewish population consists entirely of ghosts—is, of course, not unique to Kőszeg. The preservation of memory—no matter how tinged that memory may be with guilt and repentance—is, during times of economic crisis and transition, a luxury few, if any, nations can afford to indulge in.

And yet as I gaze from the innocent patio of Ernő Kolnhofer out at yet another of Eastern Europe's sad, neglected ruins, yet another endangered testimony to history's most unspeakable tragedy and evil, it occurs to me that it may also, ironically enough, be a necessity no nation can afford to pass up.

APRIL 1995

ON THE 'HUNGER'
OF JEWISH WRITERS

A speech delivered in 1994 on receipt of
the Harold U. Ribalow Prize for Fiction from
Hadassah Magazine.

New York City. It has become the subject of a certain humor among
my friends, both here and in Budapest, that I must be a writer even
more hungry for recognition than most to be willing to travel so far to
receive a prize whose value doesn't even cover the expenses incurred
in accepting it. But the hunger of writers for honor and recognition is
an old and, I think, rather tired subject, as is the cliché that the most
important things in life can't be measured in money, so I won't waste
the few precious minutes I have here by either pleading guilty to, or
defending myself against, it.

What I would rather speak about—in accepting, with great gratitude,
my half of this monetarily modest but, for me at least, hugely bountiful,
prize—is the *reason* for my willingness—indeed, eagerness—to come
so far to claim it. For anyone engaged in a lover's quarrel—as I and

21

many of those of my background and experience long have been, NOT with Judaism itself, but with our particular Jewish *experience*—lives with a certain anxiety that the quarrel will be seen as eclipsing the love, that the subject of the debate will overshadow the fact that it is only with that which one loves—as in Jacob's wrestling with the Angel—that one genuinely wishes to quarrel, in the hope that either it or oneself, hopefully both, might be improved.

This willingness to argue, I would maintain, is at the very core of Jewish experience, and, therefore, of Jewish love, though many a Jewish writer in our own time, most notably Philip Roth (and Abraham Cahan before him), has been taken to task for insisting on it. It is, however, for me, best and most poignantly exemplified in a poem by my recently deceased friend and mentor, the former Poet Laureate of the United States, Howard Nemerov, yet another somewhat "lapsed" Jew who never stopped being one. The poem is entitled "Debate with a Rabbi," and I'm happily willing to sacrifice a portion of the time I have— particularly since my own novel contains a number of such, implicit or explicit, 'debates' with rabbis—to read it to you:

DEBATE WITH A RABBI

You've lost your religion, the Rabbi said.
  It wasn't much to keep.

You should affirm the spirit
And the communal solidarity.
  I don't feel so solid, I said.

We are the people of the Book, the Rabbi said.
  Not of the phone book, said I.
Ours is a great tradition, said he,
And a wonderful history.
  But history is over, I said.

We Jews are creative people, the Rabbi said.
  Make something then, said I.
In science and in art, said he,
Violinists and physicists have we.
  Fiddle and physic indeed, I said.

THE SINS OF THE FATHERS

> Stubborn and stiff-necked man! the Rabbi cried.
> The pain you give me, said I.
> Instead of bowing down, said he,
> You go on in your obstinacy.
> We Jews are that way, I replied.

Yes, we Jews *are* that way—though there are many ideologists and moralists who would, in their own "obstinacy," argue otherwise. But, since it's the writer's business not to stand for ideologies or particular religious doctrines or moralities, but to attempt to reveal certain—both highly personal, and, hopefully, at the same time *im*personal—truths, I would like to tell you here today, on a very personal note, why my portion of the Harold U. Ribelow Prize means so much to me.

Several years ago, in an issue of *The Boston Review,* I published a first-person autobiographical essay entitled "I Remember Linda," a reminiscence of my early adolescent years in an almost entirely *yekkeh*-occupied building in Washington Heights. This essay—in which I attempted to depict, with as much emotional honesty and as great an accuracy of reminiscence as I could, the near-obsessive desire of several of the adolescent boys in our building at 801 West 181st Street (boys with names like Fleischhaker, Fleischmann, Blumenthal, Engel, and Berger) for a certain (to us) beautiful and relentlessly appealing red-haired Italian girl—the only *schiksa* in the building, of course—named Linda del Casino. This essay later became, in slightly altered form, a section of my novel *Weinstock Among the Dying*.

The theme of the essay, I believe, is an old, and perhaps tired, one: the attraction of most people—be they old, young, Jews, Christians, men, women, urban or rural—to what is exotic and forbidden. And I was simply, in the manner dictated by my own experience, trying to do that time-honored theme yet another small piece of writerly justice. I was teaching at Harvard at the time and, several weeks after the essay appeared, much to my surprise, a letter—bearing the return address of a prominent Jewish writer whom I had met, very briefly, on two occasions and whose name I most certainly won't mention here—arrived in my mailbox.

When I opened the letter, I found inside what seemed to me then, and still does, an utterly incredible diatribe, accusing me, in no uncertain terms, of the usual *schiksa*-loving Jewish self-hatred and suggesting that the women in my life (including both the Linda of my piece and my first wife, whom my correspondent had once, very briefly, met) were merely "instruments of your program, the keys to what you regard as your prison cell."

I won't go on here about this painful incident, except to say that, given that letter's angry response to my doing what I felt, and still feel, was merely my writerly, if not my ideological, duty—and the fact that virtually the same section was included in the novel this organization and its distinguished judges so generously have seen fit to honor as "a work of fiction on a Jewish theme"—I'm particularly grateful to realize that my book is not, at least to *all* Jewish eyes at, the work of yet another self-hating Jewish anti-Semite. For, as Philip Roth has said elsewhere, I too am deeply proud of my good fortune in being born, and remaining, a Jew— *"a Jew,"* as I once wrote in a poem, *"now / a Jew in the next life too"*—an experience and an identity which comprises, as Roth has written, exactly the kind of "complicated, interesting, morally demanding, and very singular experience" that makes life—for a writer at least—fascinating and worth writing about. And it is an identity which—living as I do, at this very moment, in a city and a district and a street and a building in which, just fifty years ago, history entered the houses of thousands of Hungarian Jews who survived the atrocities of the German Nazis and Hungarian Arrow Cross as they huddled in what were called *sárga csillagos házak* ("yellow star houses"), often ten and more families to a single flat, while their less fortunate relatives in the Hungarian countryside were being rounded up and taken to concentration camps—I emphatically, and without the slightest ambivalence, claim for my own.

The second anecdote I have to relate about my novel in connection with this prize is an even more personal—and even more uncannily autobiographical—one. There is another section in *Weinstock Among the Dying*—again based (though I assure you that not the entire novel is) on a personal experience—in which Martin Weinstock, as a high school boy in New York, receives, for his outstanding academic work, a $400 scholarship (the full annual tuition at the state university he is about to attend) from yet another Jewish organization, the B'nai B'rith. The award letter commends Weinstock, among other things, for the "great promise" he holds out, both for himself and for the Jewish community as a whole.

In the scene in question, Martin has been anxiously waiting for his prize money to arrive, since—given his penurious stepmother and her neurotic relationship to money—he needs it to help pay his way through school. When it fails to show up, he finally asks his father—a

psychologically wounded, highly narcissistic German-Jewish refugee—
if he's seen the check, only to have his father inform him (as, indeed,
mine once did) that, yes, the check *had* arrived, but he, on his own
initiative and without consulting his son, had decided to send it back,
because, as he puts it, *"no son von Heinz Weinstock is going to take
charity from the B'nai B'rith."*

Now, without going into any further detail about my own father,
whom I've long ago forgiven and who recently celebrated his ninetieth
birthday here in New York, let me just say that it was this scene—and,
indeed, *that* experience—which, somehow, made me all the more determined to come here personally to claim my portion of this prize. For
one of the themes of *Weinstock Among the Dying* (assuming a writer,
with the help of time, becomes merely another reader of his own book)
seems to me to be the possibility of rectifying, rather than merely repeating, the sufferings of one's childhood, the possibility that such suffering and loss can, at least momentarily, be redeemed—a theme which
is inherent in much of Jewish literature: for example, in the figure of
Lieb the baker, whose tears only serve to sweeten his bread in Bernard
Malamud's tragic and wonderful story "The Loan," or in the tragically
heroic figure of Juliek, who still somehow manages to play Beethoven
on the violin in the gas chambers of Auschwitz in Elie Wiesel's autobiographical novel *Night*.

So you can, perhaps, imagine that—as the once-young boy whose
father sent his check back to the B'nai B'rith, who has now become a
father and a man himself—I might have wanted to be here personally
this time to claim my check, before anyone had a chance to send it
back. I also wanted to say, once again, how proud and grateful I am—
because I believe, with the poet Wallace Stevens, that a writer writes,
above all, "not to a chamber of commerce, but to a gallery of one's
own"—to receive this prize from those who are, all personal ideologies
and experiences notwithstanding, "my own," and to feel, at last, that
my friend Aharon Appelfeld's words upon reading an earlier draft of
the book several years ago have finally been confirmed. "Michael," he
said to me, as he handed back the manuscript over mid-afternoon coffee in Brookline, "*such* a Jewish book."

Thank you so very, very much for this great honor. *Shalom* and God
bless you all.

DECEMBER 14, 1994

PART II

HISTORY ENTERING THE HOUSE

AND THEIR FLAGS
ARE STILL THERE

Several years ago, while rather unenthusiastically a regional finalist for a White House Fellowship during the Bush Administration (I feared a Democrat would *never* again get elected), I found myself, to my amazement, the only one among my group of male finalists *not* wearing an American flag lapel. The fact was that I had always been, and still continue to be, suspicious of flags and flag-wavers, being convinced that if patriotism isn't, as Samuel Johnson contended, the last refuge of a scoundrel, it is at the very least one of humankind's least imaginative manifestations of love of country. Patriotism, in fact—as opposed to a questioning and critical affection for one's country—always seemed to me yet another sign of that diminished sense of self demagogues and other extremists have traditionally loved to exploit.

Yet, finding myself now here in Hungary, and having already been confronted, more than periodically (on at least August 20th, October 23rd, and again just the other day on March 15th) with the tri-colored Hungarian *zászló* blowing in various commemorative winds and near-winds, I am forced, once again (as every good expatriate must) to reevaluate my prejudices, to consider them afresh from within my

WHEN HISTORY ENTERS THE HOUSE

present context. For nations with unhappy national histories, like people with unhappy childhoods, can make widely divergent uses of their past adversities—from exploiting them in order to justify their own later barbarisms (*viz.*, the Nazis with respect to the Versailles Treaty) to allowing them to create a deeper, more meaningful context for mature acts of compassion and empathy (*viz.*, the examples of Abraham Lincoln and of psychoanalyst/Holocaust survivor Viktor Frankl). It is precisely, in fact, because all feeling (and all history) is double-edged that interpretation—and, indeed, art itself—may be possible. As my father used to put it in German (and as was reflected in the behavior of a devoutly Zen Buddhist former philosophy professor of mine who, with an air of utter detachment, played the stock market), *"wenn zwei Dasselbe tun ist es nicht Dasselbe"* ("When two people—or nations—do the same thing, it is not always the same").

The other night while walking with my wife and three-year-old son in the midst of the flag-decked candlelight procession between *Bem tér* and the Castle to commemorate Hungary's ill-fated Revolution of 1848, I mused that perhaps Hungarian patriotism (not to be confused with racist-inspired and -inspiring nationalism), perhaps this, too, is a species of a different sort from America's Reagan- and Bushisms of the past twelve years, from the kind of "America: Love It or Leave It" flag-waving my own generation experienced from the far Right in the late 1960s and early '70s.

The truth is that I found myself, against all my better impulses, *moved* the other night as I stood on Castle Hill amid the peaceful crowd of candle-holders and (in far smaller numbers) flag-wavers. I was moved, perhaps, because, as an outsider, I can *afford* to be moved by the patriotism of others without the self-criticism and cynicism I direct at patriotism among my own kind. I was moved, perhaps, because of my increasing awareness that the history of Hungary is, largely, the history of a nation that has been far more dominat*ed* than dominat*ing,* far more victim*ized* than victim*izing.* I was moved, perhaps, because the final ceremony itself (a dramatic reading of poems by Vörösmarty Mihály and Petőfi Sándor followed by a concert, the combination of which felt something like the melding of a Grateful Dead concert and a Papal Mass) was, somehow, dignified and moving, resembling at moments (unlike the typically fist-thumping American patriotic pep-rally that feels, all too often, like the halftime festivities of a college football game) something not so much akin to propaganda as to prayer.

History Entering the House

And I was moved, perhaps above all, because of the fact that the candles *did* so vastly outnumber the flags, and because of my sense that—although, throughout history, all sorts of atrocities have been committed in the name of a flag—very few have ever been committed by the light of a candle...or in its gently flickering name.

March 1993

GEORGE KONRÁD:
AN APPRECIATION

"Life is good luck, death is bad luck," writes the Hungarian novelist George Konrád—who, to our own good fortune as well as his own, turns sixty on April 2nd—speaking in the voice of his literary alter-ego David Kobra in Konrád's fourth novel, *A Feast in the Garden,* published in English in 1992.

Such a statement—tossed off, perhaps carelessly, by a lesser writer, or glossed over dismissively by an unvigilant reader—carries, one soon comes to realize, a prophetic weight in Konrád's *oeuvre:* He *knows.* He has been there: "Out of 200 of my schoolmates, only seven of us survived," he recalls in the same chapter—not with what he has questioningly described elsewhere as the "egocentricity of the survivor," but with the simply stated near-detachment of one who has been both witness and participant, one who has *earned,* through toil and experience, his way to the deep resonances of his own deceptively un-simple simplicities.

Konrád, the best-known abroad of contemporary Hungarian authors, is that great (a word I use with an appropriate reticence) thing among writers—the profoundly moral man (or woman) who is not a moralist. Nazis and "high priest[s] of frivolity," as David describes his uncle Arnold

Kobra, cohabit in his novels, because they cohabit in our lives (and sometimes, alas, in the same person) as well. For Konrád—as for Musil, Mann, Chekhov, Kundera, even Proust—there is no easy, sentimental refuge in the somber: He takes, rather, as a friend of mine once put it, the somber out of the serious. Surrounded—as Konrád has been for much of his life—by the dark vicissitudes of history and politics, the modern truism that the powers of evil have so often made both literal and psychological mincemeat of the powers of goodness, it is neither death nor resignation that Konrád's characters embrace, but—as Flaubert once put it—"Life! Life! To have erections!"

"You know, my dear," Arnold Kobra replies to his daughter Klára when she asks him why he needed to have so many lovers, "when we get undressed, everything is discovered. Maybe that's what we want, discovery."

And that is, indeed, what the bulk of Konrád's characters—and, we suspect, Konrád himself—most want: *discovery*...of sex, of love, of food, of human companionship in all its mixed and often botched complexity. Because Konrád, as he described himself in 1989, is "the kind of stubborn optimist [who] thinks of our presence as more decisive than our annihilation," who is willing, despite all he knows of human darkness and what is often individual powerlessness in the face of it, to have a seat at the table, to partake of *The Feast in the Garden*.

It is this ongoing hunger for life, this resonant conviction that there is, ultimately, something good and inextinguishable in humankind and its enterprises, that makes of both Konrád the man and Konrád the writer (the divergence between the two, as with all such profoundly authentic figures, being slight) such dual treasures—in any language—for our time. As the first Central European President of PEN International, as one of the leaders of the Democratic Charter here in Hungary, as a man for whom small and personal acts of kindness—those "minute particulars" Blake spoke of—need not pose themselves as adversarial to the larger, public acts the times may require, Konrád is not someone who needs to pause and ask for whom the bell tolls. He knows: it tolls for us all.

"Why should I as a writer stick my nose into political matters?" he has asked elsewhere (*Antipolitics,* 1984). "Because they frighten me.... We live in a crabbed society, and what I am most interested in is how we can make it less crabbed."

I could pretend—perhaps, it occurs to me, I am already pretending—to be a longtime admirer, or a close friend, of Konrád's, neither of which would be true. I have come, in fact, to his work both backwards

History Entering the House

(beginning with "The High Prince of Frivolity" chapter of *A Feast in the Garden* that was excerpted, last year, in *The New Yorker,* and moving on from there to *The Loser* (1982), *The City Builder* (1977), and *The Case Worker* (1974)) and lately. But mine, as I suspect almost anyone's would be who discovers his work, is the enthusiasm of the freshly converted, the passion of the younger writer who has found in the voice of one older, wiser, more profoundly talented and humane than himself, a model for what redeems us both as artists and as members of humankind. A feast awaits all those who have not yet sat at his bountiful table. And, with these small, inadequate encomiums of praise, I will allow him, as we should always allow our betters, the last word (from a 1989 essay, "Show Me Your Eyes"):

> Perhaps the day will come when the Messiah steals past under our windows and history quickens its pace in his wake. Then minds will come to live, strange encounters multiply, the grip of routine will be broken and every day will bring us something new. Then students will take each other's arms so tightly that they can no longer be easily separated. The smile that will fill the whole city will swallow the threats. Perhaps the day will dawn when the schoolchildren show evidence of accelerating progress in the one crucial subject of the human school: understanding each other. And the unknown Messiah, walking the pavements, with his well-worn briefcase under his arm, will not consider whether the man whose forehead he touches is a Jew, a Christian, or a Muslim, he will only look to see what there is in his eyes.

Such a man, it seems to me, and such a writer, deserves to be wished *boldog születésnapot!*—a Happy Birthday!—from us all.

APRIL 1993

WHEN HISTORY
ENTERS THE HOUSE

Fellow citizens, we cannot escape history.

ABRAHAM LINCOLN
MESSAGE TO CONGRESS
DECEMBER 1, 1862

"History entered the house," says a character in George Konrád's *A Feast in the Garden* when a World War II Russian tank drives right through the wall of his house. And history, indeed, has entered through the doors, walls, and windows of Hungarian houses for centuries now— a pleasant stage-set, perhaps, from a purely literary point of view, but a serious intrusion on those who, like Konrád, would "prefer the state to be like the management of a good hotel." In other words: efficient, unobtrusive, facilitating one's pleasures and comforts without drawing undue attention to itself.

From where my family lives, virtually across from Hősök tere on Dózsa György út, history also enters the house—not exactly through the walls, but through the windows, from which we look out on the brightly lit white billboard that announces for all the world to see:

**ITT ÁLLTA
REGNUM MARIANUM
TEMPLOM**

**RÁKOSI MÁTYÁS 1951-BAN
LEROMBOLTATTA**

In plain English: "On this site once stood the Catholic church destroyed by Mátyás Rákosi in 1951." "My grandfather was executed under Rákosi," my friend, the poet Péter Kántor, told me one evening when he came to our house and gazed at the sign from our window. "My parents were married in that church," said our friend Benedek, looking out at the same sign. "It was right in front of this window," Konrád told me the night he and his wife Judit came over for dinner and stood on our balcony, "that Tito spoke the last time he was in Budapest." *History enters the house.* Yes, history enters the house.

On the morning of October 23rd, the anniversary of the '56 Revolution, we gazed out the same window to find that a stage—with a large, satirical bust of Stalin and another of a massive, sickle-bedecked Soviet boot mounted on it—had been erected for a demonstration sponsored by István Csurka's *Magyar Fórum*. And since then, from time to time, we've looked out at a variety of demonstrations and marches—pro and contra Horthy's reburial, pro and contra the Hungarian media situation, pro and contra a wide variety of other contemporary Hungarian political issues. In fact, every time we look out from our balcony, or open the front door to let in a Hungarian friend, it seems that—though often somewhat tragically, as it is prone to—history enters the house.

Yet, Konrád's understandable wish (particularly given his own history) for a likeness between a nation and a smoothly functioning hotel notwithstanding, we cannot, as Lincoln suggested, escape our nation's history—any more than we can escape our own—and it becomes, perhaps, instead a question of whether that history is written by tanks or by television, by Hitler or by Hollywood, by sages or by screenwriters, whether the "medicine" it administers enters raucously and painfully, like a tank, or benignly and subliminally, like a commercial. For history is always with us—the subtext, the thin, often imperceptible sheaf, upon which all personal history, like it or not, is written.

So that, after some eighteen months of living in Hungary, it was perhaps no accident that—while recently staying at a hotel in my own nation's capital (Washington, D. C.)—I felt a certain sense of expectant *déja vu,* a certain premonition that, here too, history was about to enter my house, when I suddenly saw a bright swath of floodlights illuminating the Georgetown streets and heard voices echoing from a series of bullhorns. I ran to my hotel window to find, to my amazement, a huge crowd of mainly young people lining several blocks of Georgetown's main drag, M Street. *Ah ha!,* I thought, here too—in this nation of mine in which (according to John Updike) the State is no more intrusive than the daily visit of the mailman—history enters the house.

"What's all the commotion about?" I asked a young couple munching pizza in front of my hotel after I had run down the stairs. Having, already perhaps, too much of Central Europe in my veins, I expected it was, at the very least, a spontaneous appearance by President Clinton, or a ticker-tape parade in support of the Brady Bill, that had so urgently summoned the masses onto the streets, that had so brightly illuminated this otherwise somber November night.

But this, I was suddenly harshly reminded, was America, not Budapest—America, where history has all the (obvious) impact of a deep breath beneath the din of Hollywood, where the voices of sages are drowned out by the floppy discs of screenwriters, years of testimony and analysis by the Warren Commission rendered void by three hours of Oliver Stone. "It's Arnold Schwarzenegger!" the wildly expectant twosome told me. "He's shooting a scene from his new movie."

And there, sure enough, right before me—like De Gaulle triumphantly re-entering Paris in April of 1945, like Havel victoriously waving from the balcony of Prague Castle in the winter of '89—was none other than the great Terminator himself, Arnold Schwarzenegger, who, having terminated my dreams, had brought (I realized as I went back to my room, shut the window, and crawled into bed) history into the house once again.

NOVEMBER 1993

ON THE LONELINESS OF HUNGARIANS

Loneliness is destiny…

SÁNDOR MÁRAI

What's lonely and speaks a language hardly anyone else in the world understands? If you've answered "a Hungarian," most Hungarians themselves would say you're correct.

For few nationalities on this earth have been more intimate with the oxymoronic companionship of loneliness than Hungarians, and very few Hungarians have known more about that lonely and inexhaustible subject than Sándor Márai, the recently rediscovered (because once again published) Hungarian novelist, playwright, and essayist whose marvelous autobiographical memoir, *Föld! Föld! (Land! Land!)* is soon to be issued in English jointly by Corvina and the C. E. U. Press.

Marai, an ardent anti-communist and defender of middle-class humanistic ideals who committed suicide in San Diego in 1989, left Hungary for political reasons in September of 1948, having bequeathed to his homeland and his mother tongue some forty-six books, mostly novels. From exile in Switzerland, Italy and the United States, he added a further sixteen titles, all in Hungarian, read almost exclusively by an intellectual elite of his own generation who were able to slip his books past customs officials on rare visits to the West. Unlike many of his brethren-in-exile, Márai never returned to Hungary, even for a visit, and even after the easing of censorship and other restrictions in the 1970s.

Already feeling suffocated by the political situation under Horthy and the growing threats of German fascism, Márai wrote in his *1943-44 Journal* that "in Hungary, one can live only in internal emigration. By turning completely inward, toward my work. By emigrating into my work." The quintessential artist, Márai experienced loneliness as not merely a *characteristic* of being Hungarian but as nearly an *equivalence* to it:

> The consciousness that being Hungarian meant the same as being lonely, that the Hungarian language was incomprehensible and unrelated to other languages, that the "Hungarian" phenomenon consisting of diverse races but still typically Hungarian was also foreign to those who were next-door neighbors and shared a common fate with the Hungarians for a thousand years—there was something benumbing in this consciousness. Sometimes, for a brief period, at times of shifting currents of civilization, hopefulness befogged this feeling of loneliness. But it did not last long.

Unlike, for example, Gertrude Stein, an exile who reveled in a certain (though not equivalent) linguistic isolation, Márai's experience of linguistic loneliness seems somehow generically Hungarian: The subconscious consolation available to English-speaking exiles like Stein—

the sense that English is somehow nonetheless the readily available *lingua franca* of modern culture—was never available to him or to other Hungarians. Speaking, rather, of the twin isolations of history and language, Márai felt there were "no other people…still living in Europe that were as stifled by loneliness as the Hungarians…. The 'people,' like the individual, knew that this loneliness could not be altered, because it was destined." Hungarian loneliness, according to him, was "a shortness of breath, an asthmatic lack of air," a loneliness unlike any other loneliness.

But Márai also knew that loneliness, while a source of great suffering, could also be a source of great strength, a strength to which Hungarian history and culture have repeatedly testified. "As is always the case with loneliness," he observed, "the 'Hungarian' could only hope for an ally within himself, inward." Loneliness, Márai acknowledged, does not bestow happiness. "But the loneliness of Hungary," he added,

> was a source of strength, an oasis in the European desert. With its fate, its good and bad characteristics, a people was left tragically on its own between East and West…. Some continued to hope. Others were silent for long periods of time. Then, because they could not do anything else, they set about fashioning order in the loneliness.

And so it well may be that what all too often are mistaken by outsiders for Hungarian sullenness or pessimism are merely the outward manifestations of that seemingly fated inner alliance—the alliance of Hungarians with that which has most deeply, and most reliably, earned their trust: their own solitary selves. When one thinks about Hungary, and about Hungarian culture, in this way—as a kind of ordered, and dignified, loneliness—one is able, perhaps, to move away from cliché and stereotype and see, instead, a merely human people, in all their joy and pain, in all their merely human loneliness.

MARCH 1996

PART III

HUNGARIAN SOULS

George Konrád in the garden of his house
in Hegymagas, Hungary, July 1996.

A CONVERSATION
WITH GEORGE KONRÁD

It was a quote from Konrád's *A Feast in The Garden* to the effect that "most writers write falsely about love because they are afraid of their wives. Behind every writer stands an Argus-eyed marital censor."—that triggered the genesis of my own present novel-in-progress, in which I soon found Konrád himself making an appearance as a character. It being no simple thing to telephone a character in one's own still-unfinished novel, much less a writer one so deeply admires, I waited some five months after first arriving in Budapest in late August of 1992 to finally call Konrád and suggest that we get together.

We met for the first time on December l8, 1992, in the 15th-floor bar of the Hotel Budapest, one of Konrád's favorite meeting places for its spectacular view of the Danube, downtown Pest, and the Buda hills (notwithstanding how hideously unattractive the circular 1950-ish building is from the outside), where Konrád was just finishing an interview with several Romanian radio journalists. Several months later, we met again with both our families (including Konrád's wife Judit and their two young sons) at Konrád's apartment. I returned to Konrád's house to borrow some books a few days later when a black-leather-jacketed young man showed up, uninvited, after having hitchhiked all the way from Slovakia to ask if the novelist (who had never met the man) would write him a reference to attend the university and study arts administration. Konrád, ever-generous, agreed, remarking to me afterwards that he probably shouldn't have done so, but that the young man seemed "decent enough." It was at our fourth meeting, on a gorgeous, blossom-rich Budapest morning in Konrád's basement studio in late April, 1993—after Konrád poured us both a generous glass of Russian vodka and lit a cigarette—that the following conversation took place:

MB: *I was thinking this morning, since you have just come back from the meeting of the International PEN Club, of which you're the first Central European president, of something my friend the Polish essayist Tomas Lubienski said in a talk he gave recently here in Budapest. Speaking of the Central European intellectual and his or her penchant for meetings and the like, Lubienski said,*

> *They all escape even more comfortably into the world of round-tables, symposia and sessions, which usually take place in the more beautiful parts of the world, beautiful as if to compensate for the fact that the matters raised at them are so often unpleasant. The frequency of these meetings, their budget and significance rise in parallel to the rise in the evil with which they deal. Think how many fruitful contacts have resulted from the threat to democracy in Central Europe. Or xenophobia, which is a universal theme for the whole continent. If those who fulminate at these meetings could actually get through to the xenophobes or populists then the intello would lose the reason for these constant trips.*

GK: [Laughs.] It's right and it's quite funny what your friend wrote and I could say even more about that, I could say that conferences are for conferences and it is in the nature of the eternal professional life of intellectuals to meet, to talk, to talk, to talk; that is their—how to say?—their sickness.

MB: *Yes,* la maladie.

GK: And it's, of course, evident that they don't go to the most ugly places. Actually we were just in some of the most beautiful places—in Dubrovnik and Var - but I wouldn't say that they are without their problems. And it is a long story, which I don't want to bore you with, but somehow the conflicts of the world also reoccur within the PEN Club. And these are solvable only though compromise in order to keep the PEN Club—that world community of writers which, however, is useful because it sometimes helps to get people out of prison, and somehow also has a kind of authority, a kind of spirit—together.

MB: *I was thinking of this, perhaps, because you yourself say in* The Loser—*or, rather, your narrator says, "I will always find reasons not to be where I am. And it's always better if these reasons are morally compelling."*

GK: I'm one person when I'm a novelist and another person when I perform the duties of a position. And these are not the same. I look at Mr. Konrád from the corner of the room.

MB: *So that the man who writes and the man who speaks...*

GK: Yes, the man who writes and the man who presides are not the same. I try also in *The Caseworker* to look at the social worker from that same corner of the room. Or I do the same with a sci-fi planner in *The City Builder,* or with the former politician, the defeated intellectual, in *The Loser*. So I try to keep a distance from roles I have created for their action, because action is one thing, and to come together and talk in a public arena is another.

MB: *And yet this conflict—between action and intellection—seems to me one of the great conflicts intellectuals have and one of the reasons intellectuals, perhaps especially in Central Europe, are drawn to politics and simultaneously go to such great lengths to disclaim any interest in it, to insist that their involvement is reluctant. As, for example, in the case of Havel or Vargas-Llosa...or, to some extent, yourself.*

GK: Yes, because it's a normal ambiguity and paradox. And we can't avoid these paradoxes. Because, after all, why are we involved or interested? Because John Updike can very easily say, and in a funny way, that for him the state actually means nothing more than the mailbox. But for an average Hungarian writer, the state didn't mean the mailbox—it meant all kinds of possible dangers he had to confront or adapt to or avoid or face. There were many strategies, many possible strategies, but people were *forced* to have a strategy and those who avoided the hot issues had a politics as well, because they knew precisely what they were avoiding. As for myself, I'm more a type of candid *facing* person, so I don't try too much to avoid things, because that's also uncomfortable.

MB: *The avoidance is uncomfortable?*

GK: Yes. The avoidance is uncomfortable because, for instance, let's say there is a Western journalist. And he comes and asks me, let's say ten years ago: "Mr. Konrád, what do you think about this or that?" If I answer truthfully, and if he publishes my answer in his newspaper, then I will not be published. It's quite simple. Therefore the great, great majority of writers said, "Oh, I'm terribly busy. Oh, I'm not interested in politics. Oh, I know nothing about it," and so on. So these questions, which were simple questions, very direct and simple questions, were in fact provocative questions. And it was a collective self-defense mechanism not to face these so-called provocative questions. I didn't do that because it was somehow uncomfortable for me, but it meant that I was a banned author for fifteen years. But I would say that many writers who were maybe a little bit smarter than I was could publish, so they could find their way.

MB: *Writers who were more willing, perhaps, to compromise, or who found, one might argue, a slyer way around the censure.*

GK: Yes, yes. But I would say that all of them, with all kinds of different personal strategies, took account of the conditions and knew what type of way they had to choose for their own sake. And therefore I would say that political decisions were characteristic of everyone.

MB: *Which is what, for example, Miklós Haraszti wrote about in* The Velvet Prison.

GK: Yes. But let me go back to what I was saying about Updike. I was asked by a Dutch journalist, "What is your wish?" And I said: To have such a dull society as you. Where the politics is so much like the management of a good hotel. I don't care who the director of the hotel is, as long as the service is O.K. and they don't come to my room and search my papers.

MB: *You said somewhere—again in* The Loser, *I believe—that the less one is aware of the state the better off they are. Now, you mention Updike and his anecdote of the mailbox. And, of course, most of us in America are not terribly aware of the state on a daily basis. I mean we know Clinton is President and not Bush, but it doesn't go much further than that for many Americans.*

GK: But the fact that your personal situation doesn't depend too much on the person of the president doesn't mean that in your existential life you won't feel it.

MB: *At the same time, I suppose that one of the attractions we in the West now feel for contemporary Eastern European literature is precisely this impingement of history and politics on daily life...beyond the mailbox. You have an anecdote somewhere in A Feast in the Garden of a butcher into whose house a tank suddenly drove, and you quote him as saying, "History entered the house," or something like that. So, for the Eastern European writer, history has always entered the house; history has always interfered with private life. Yet not so acutely for us.*

GK: Yes. So, for instance, I taught the continental novel in the U. S. and I had a bright student, a very reasonable young American guy. And the subject was Kafka's *The Trial*. And he said, "I don't understand this man. He's under arrest, sure, but he can always move. Why doesn't he just emigrate to the U. S.? Why does he allow himself to be subjected to these authorities?"

MB: [Laughs.] *But I think this is part of the very attraction, and in a way the ambivalence, of these relationships. Updike, I think, provides a very good example. Take his character Rabbit Angstrom. In some sense one might say that if someone, a hundred years from now, wanted to know what middle-class life in suburban America was like in the latter half of the 20th Century, he or she might look to the Rabbit novels. Yet a frequent criticism of Updike—not one I share, but a frequent criticism—is that Rabbit is a character without moral depth—a Toyota dealer whose main issues in life are infidelity, his waning sexuality and physical prowess, and the typical middle-class family saga...but without any deep connection to the larger society. Whereas the very attractiveness of Eastern European characters to a Western (particularly an American) mind, I think, is that history is always entering the house.*

GK: Yes. Once I met with some students in Colorado. They were a mixed group, but all Western students. And they said, "You know, we have a kind of envy for you because you have *decisions* in your life. And, until now, we haven't had decisions with any internal drama." So the rational decisions of a career are not thought of as real decisions. And the problems here [in Central Europe] are really another type of problem, but maybe it's still a transitory situation.

MB: *I think of what Nadasda Mandelstam said at one point in* Hope Against Hope. *She said, "we longed for the ordinary un-happinesses, we longed for divorce and infidelity and the like...." So now you are in a society which at least aspires to, and seems to be in a period of transition toward, these ordinary unhappinesses. In other words, you can no longer entirely say, as Philip Roth once said about Eastern and Western literature, that in the West everything is allowed and nothing is dangerous, while in the East nothing is allowed and everything is dangerous. Now a great deal is permitted. You are published widely. I no longer need to go to the room full of "banned books" in the Széchényi Library to look for your work.*

GK: Yes, yes. But, you know, I wouldn't say that the dangers have disappeared from this society. They merely have a new face. For instance, I could take into account, with a certain amount of rational risk of a dictatorship, what I knew during the Communist period. Now, however, those who might be dangerous are foolish people who have some ideological motivation to do foolish things. For example, there are in the Balkan countries today, extremist groups who will probably go the way of the death squads. And perhaps such extremists will bring a certain amount of violence into this sphere. For instance, I have never before received as many dirty, aggressive, and menacing letters as I receive now. I won't go so far as to say that there is a short road from these letters to actions. It's a quite long way, and these are generally anonymous letters.

MB: *From Hungarians?*

GK: From Hungarians. And they are, on the one hand, very obscene, very anti-Semitic, and extremely vulgar and aggressive.

MB: *And, aside from this anti-Semitism, do they share any particular content?*

GK: That I should leave the country.

MB: *I remember, in your introduction to Haraszti's* The Velvet Prison, *where you talk about Haraszti as a young man and you say that, at one point, you said to him, "Miki, go away from here. This is not a good place for you." And you then write—and this was 1986— "I've learned by now that he will never leave. He wants to prove it here...his truth." Well, you also didn't leave and I assume don't have any intention of doing so.*

GK: No, I will never leave.

MB: *And yet someone like Haraszti—whom you refer to as kind of a "younger brother"—has taken a very different path—he's a politician now, a member of Parliament.*

GK: Yes, you know, sometimes I have a kind of anxiety for some friends, although I face this anxiety in my own case. But it's a little bit the way I am with my children when they climb up onto a very high rock or wall, and I'm terribly afraid that they will fall down, although I'm not nearly as afraid for myself when I climb up onto the same place. In Haraszti's case, it's another thing, since in certain periods he was in real danger. But I don't want to talk more about that right here. *[At this point, Konrád asks me to turn off the tape and reveals something to me in private, something which, I'm forced to remind him, he'd also mentioned publicly in his earlier introduction to Haraszti's book.]*

MB: [Turns on the tape once again.] *You are now, I think, quite a popular writer in the West, though I can only speak for the States. You are published by a major publisher [Harcourt, Brace], reviewed in* The New York Times, The New York Review of Books, *and* The New Republic, *and published in* The New Yorker. *At least in Germany, you are widely translated, and you received the* Friedenspreis *(Peace Prize) of the German Booksellers' Association just last year. So it seems fair to say that you are now quite well known in the West.*

And yet I have a sense from talking to some of your countrymen that you—as Timothy Garton Ash also mentions in his book, The Uses of Adversity—*are not quite considered as representative of Hungarian literature by your fellow Hungarians as you are in the West. It's very hard for me, an outsider, to gauge this, and I can also see—just judging from the festivities at your sixtieth birthday celebration the other week—that you are quite beloved by your countrymen. Yet I have a sense that by many Hungarians you are considered as predominantly a political theorist, and that perhaps your books are thought of as insufficiently narrative to be "literature." Which is one of their attractions, I think, not only for myself, but for the West in general, where we hunger for a certain aphoristic "wisdom." Do you think it is true that you are less appreciated here than in the West? And, if so, why?*

GK: I can't speak a lot about that, I don't know, and I don't like to speak about views of my own work. It's not my job. You need to talk with other people about that.

MB: *Well, let me put it another way, because I am curious about a certain aspect of this. I think it was Carlos Fuentes who, in his introduction to* The City Builder, *called you an oracular, rather than an apocalyptic, writer. And it's this very aphoristic, oracular quality that I think of as a source of your work's attractiveness. I love this in writers, and I think it's why we're attracted to writers like Kundera, or to Proust for that matter, or to Thomas Mann. But, on the other hand, I suppose it can be said of your novels that the narrative quality is sometimes difficult to gauge.*

GK: Yes, sure, it's not a real plot at work in them. So, if you require a normal, brave plot, you won't find it there. In that sense, they are bad novels.

MB: *In America, on the other hand, there's so much talk about narrative. Students, for example, are often taught about narrative structure, or—if they are writing students—the plotting of narratives. Don't you think that this more or less total absence of linear narrative is characteristic of contemporary Central European literature in general?*

GK: You know, when I was in the U. S. and was tired in the evening, I went down to the family room and watched movies on television— sometimes three movies, one after the other. They all had fantastic plots. They were worked like machines, full of good procedures. And actually they were all very mediocre movies. So it is now the job of movies to have such good and tricky plots.

MB: *So you think that, in some evolutionary sense of the genres, it's no longer the job of literature.*

GK: It doesn't interest me. And the books which have a really clear plot generally are too long for the pleasure they offer. At least for me, but I'm a bad reader—a bad novelist, a bad reader, so we shouldn't speak about that.

MB: *Well, as a bad reader, then, what American writers do you read or admire? What do you think of the condition of American literature? I have to say for myself that I feel a certain alienation from American literature, and so one of my attractions to the work of Eastern Europeans is precisely this absence of plot, precisely the things I'm asking you about. But I wonder whether, coming at it from the other direction, you read any contemporary American writers?*

GK: Yes, sometimes. I even love to read partial texts—some pages, some chapters, actually not whole books—by good colleagues. By Donald Barthelme, even by Pynchon (it's not so easy, but I use a dictionary), John Barth. I even enjoy this other type of literature by Don DeLillo, or William Burroughs.

MB: *Everyone you mentioned might be classified as a kind of innovator in American literature, all rather unconventional in their work.*

GK: We can go back further, and then I would say William Faulkner, almost everything by him. Or Flannery O'Connor.

MB: *You said somewhere else that "Russian literature saved my life." What did you mean by that? Was there any particular book? I know, of course, there is a certain great debate which rages among many Eastern European intellectuals—Dostoyevski or Tolstoy?*

GK: [Laughs.] I am for both of them. I even wanted to teach *War and Peace* and *The Brothers Karamazov* in the same course while I was in the States. You know, a French hero of the 19th-century novel is interested in his career. He would like to make it. Rastignac stands on the hill of Montmartre and looks down on Paris and says, *"A nous deux maintenant"*: "Now we come, here is our duel, I will make it." Or if he is a little bit weaker, then he won't make it. And you have all kinds of variety around this struggle of career—how to become prestigious, or rich, how to have great and high-ranking lovers. So the context of these novels is the mundane sphere, as with the little ambiguities and gossips and pains of mundane life in the wonderful Proust novels. But the *noveaux romanciers* write to the objectality of modern consumer society, without metaphysics. They push out the person, push out the choice. Within the existentialist novel, there were still some elements of free choice, but it was linked to a type of French politics which became abstract.

Stendhal is perhaps my greatest love. But in all the giants of Russian literature, you have universal, ethical issues being addressed, and also a great pendulum moving between the sensual and God. And the passions still can't identify their target. Maybe Chekhov's "Three Sisters" would like to go to Moscow. They have a desire to reach something even they cannot really define, or to have a meaningful life, or not to be *vishni*—a Russian word which means superfluous, useless. They have this terrible feeling that they are useless. Or, if you go back to the origins, it is Gogol. In Gogol, you find all the later absurdist views. You find the precursor of Kafka.

As for plot and narrative, I would say that *Crime and Punishment* is the most wonderfully constructed plot, whose strange mastery lies in the fact that the reader knows from the beginning who the murderer was. And yet from beginning to end there are all kinds of suspense—the encirclement of Raskolnikov, of the individual, and his tendencies to give himself up, or to hide, or to defend himself, and the game he plays with the prosecutor. This is a real game; it's a plot, but a different type of plot, where it is not interesting *who* the murderer was, but *what* the murderer does afterwards. As in *Anna Karenina* it is not the issue whether the marriage will end. Because a normal, decent middle-class novel begins with the first appointment, the first rendezvous, and ends with the marriage. But *Anna Karenina* begins when the marriage is already disintegrating.

MB: *You mention the passions and this yearning for God which the passions embody. One of the things I find most interesting about the Central and Eastern European novel—the novels of Kundera and Klima and Gombrowitz and yourself, or Nabokov, writing in America, among others—as opposed to most American novels, is the connection, not merely between sex and politics, but between sexual and metaphysical concerns. The fact that the lives and the passions and the characters' other yearnings seem inextricably linked. In a long monologue in* The City Builder, *for example, you say, "I don't want a city where what I detest is a duty and what I love is immoral…where if I love one human being I cannot love another, and my body, if it desires another body, must feign shame …etc., etc." A city, it seems to me, like Budapest in many ways— containing not only a wonderfully messy disorder, but which also contains a deep sensuality, a certain passion, as opposed to—for me, at least—a city like Boston. But you relate this kind of passion to both physical* and *metaphysical circumstances—it belongs not only to the life of a city, but also to the sensual lives of characters like Arnold Kobra [in* A Feast in the Garden*] which are very rich from within a great deal of metaphysical and physical despair.*

GK: You know, energies always find their way. And it's a banal truth that, in a war situation, there is always a lot of turmoil on the love scene. And if the possibilities of people to express themselves, to move around, were somehow limited, then there was a kind of underground life, an underground sexual life on the part of the whole society. In those places where women and men worked together and discipline was not too rigorous, for example, couples would leave and go for a rendezvous in town, or at the apartments of friends. So people wanted less prescribed expressions of themselves, and they found them in these many relationships. And I would say that it was quite easy to find such links between friends, and across the two Budapests—these cross relationships where everyone was somehow "in a family connection" to each another. Probably it's over. Probably it's over, even because of all the recent changes.

MB: *And so now there will be only the bland, bourgeoisified erotic life of the West?*

GK: [Laughs.] Yes, probably.

MB: *I think you said somewhere also that we—the visitors—have the abstractions and you, the permanent residents, have the ulcers. And I think it's very hard for anybody to judge this situation from outside.*

GK: But you are now in it!

MB: *Well, I'm partially in and partially, by definition, out. But I talk to many people. And there are many answers one gets, many points of view, among which one that I hear frequently these days is a kind of nostalgia for the censor.*

GK: For the censor?

MB: *Yes, for the censor. Because the life of an artist was better under socialism, some say. The state had good taste; artists were well supported. Now, the consuming public has bad taste, the trashy literature of the West is everywhere, the artist can no longer afford the cafés; everything is permitted, so the sort of coy devices of censured literature are no longer available or useful, etc., etc. And so there seems to be a certain nostalgia.*

GK: Yes, because all types of lives have their consolations. And it would be a farce to believe that everyone was constantly unhappy under communism. Actually for many intellectuals it was an acceptable life.

MB: *You yourself wrote, I think in* Antipolitics, *that "it was the best we could hope for, to achieve an enlightened paternalistic authoritarianism accompanied by a measured willingness to undertake gradual liberal reforms."*

GK: In communism itself, within communism.

MB: *So you meant only at that particular point. Do you now feel any of the nostalgia I was speaking of?*

GK: I don't feel it at all. And I believe that it's a price that a society has to pay that people can buy whatever books they want. If they want to buy bad books, I'm not authorized to hinder them.

MB: *What about your own work? How have these changes affected it?, Your last novel,* A Feast in the Garden, *must have been finished around '89. Interestingly enough, the period of that book, perhaps in some ways anticipating the end of communism, no longer deals with the socialist state as much as with the Nazi state. It's a novel more about that period than the post-war era.*

GK: Yes, actually it's also the first part of a trilogy, so it goes further in the coming volumes. And, yes, probably there is intellectually a kind of forecast in it. Because I felt that the real alternative for the bulk of the intelligentsia was not liberalism, but nationalism.

MB: *The real alternative?*

GK: To communism. Because there is a type of pendulum movement in this part of Europe between communism and nationalism, both of which are tendencies on the part of intellectuals who will ultimately get jobs with the state if their ideology wins.

MB: *As we are now in some sense already seeing.*

GK: Yes, sure. Now there is a growing bourgeoisie and therefore one part of the intellectuals are trying to create good relationships to the rich and to receive sponsorship from them for intellectual enterprises and newspapers and reviews and other publications. It was actually a great achievement that a new political class was created here. And many lawyers, doctors, physicians, historians, economists and entrepreneurs and all kinds of other people entered this political class. But now the wagon is full. And many intellectuals also went into business—mostly, by the way, Communist intellectuals.

MB: *Not unpredictably, I suppose.*

WHEN HISTORY ENTERS THE HOUSE

GK: Yes, so the former censors are now probably representatives of American firms. [Laughs.]

MB: *Yes, it's in a way very predictable, but it's also very comical.*

GK: It was predictable, yes, it's comical, it's grotesque; but what should we say? It's normal, because they have their relationships, their networks, and they are useful. And probably they were once activists, and began their careers another way. But now there is a new way, and they move in that direction.

MB: *I can't really gauge this as an outsider very well, but, to this day, when I go to Germany and see someone over, say, sixty, I can't help thinking to myself, "Where was he or she, say, in 1944?" So now this question, of course, must be prevalent here: "Where were you prior to '89?" I wonder, though, how prevalent? I notice it even at the university, for example. And it's very interesting to me because American university life also has its politics, but it is usually petty, institutional politics. But here you suddenly discover that the person whose office is next to yours, and whom you never see, is now working for the education ministry; or the person who's now the department chairman was in the ministry. And all this in an English department!*

GK: There's a greater social mobility, I would say, and it can also provide an interesting picture of the different biographies, because there is probably a psychological or moral continuity within them. So it's quite funny, for example, how former brave conformist Communists are now brave conformist nationalists. And those who were very loyal to the government are again very loyal to the government. For instance in such institutions as *Magyar Rádió*, the people who were the forerunners of the reform movement and of the critical period of the free speech movement underwent a kind of emancipation when they pushed away the internal censorship apparatus, and were really free to do what they want. Now, they aren't any longer.

MB: *In this new system, will the intellectuals who supported democracy, ironically enough, have less power because there will be a respectable bourgeoisie that no longer needs them?*

GK: Yes, yes. There is a very different type of new bourgeoisie. For instance, there is a very good restaurant in Budapest, a very expensive restaurant, and the owner of it is a new bourgeois who was probably previously a waiter, and now has become a rich person and has *several* restaurants. And he was recently asked to become a supporting member of the Hungarian PEN Club. And he became a supporting member, making a very generous "membership donation" to the Club. So there are those who have a kind of snobbism, and those who went from the former intelligentsia into the business world and, not being that skillful at it, have a bad feeling that they are now doing something really different from what they wanted to do when they were young. And that bad feeling, they feel, is somehow compensated for by their sponsorship.

MB: *I want to move away from politics, at least explicitly, for a moment and get back to literature. Czeslaw Milosz said some years ago that the problem with Western writers as opposed to writers in the East is that the former haven't been kicked in the ass enough. I suppose by this he meant that their lives have been too complacent, and I suppose there is some truth to that, since the typical career of a writer in the States these days—I would say probably not the best writers, but a fairly typical career—is the academic career, in which one is in a writing program and teaches this odd animal called Creative Writing, and so on. Do you think that this sort of life, in America particularly (I don't think Western Europe yet shares this situation), is somehow too existentially and morally empty, too complacent, for the making of great literature?*

GK: I'm not sure that every American writer needs to enclose himself within the academic world. Maybe it's easier, or reasonable, because there are jobs for creative writing teachers or writers in residence and so on. But, for example, when I was teaching in Colorado, students frequently showed me their short stories, and the young person among them who was the most gifted was the poorest one, someone on a state scholarship whose mother was a grade school teacher and who didn't have a father and who lived in a trailer. And he worked every vacation at construction. And wrote the best short stories. Because he had a much larger range of knowledge of American life, and his were very powerful texts. So probably even the United States is far more interesting than from the viewpoint of people on a campus.

But, in fact, what keeps any American citizen from walking around the world outside of the U. S.? Though I'm not sure that the type of political tourism many people undertake is the best way. Now they travel to Bosnia for two weeks, etc., etc. So this desire to visit "the outside world" for some new spiritual ammunition is now probably entering a new chapter—to go to the East in search of nationalism. I believe that even certain Jews will do that. To justify their own Jewishness, they would like to support all kinds of nationalism in Eastern Europe, and of course they will choose their favorite nationalism. But I feel that it is just as superficial as the former moods were, when people jumped from Maoism to Solzhenizinism.

MB: *In America now there is actually a name for this genre— "the literature of witness," the idea being that the writer's obligation— especially for American writers not actively engaged in politics—is simply to bear witness. Some years ago, for example, one of the few books of poetry with any popular following (in the sense that it sold more than two or three thousand copies) was a book of poems by Carolyn Forché called* The Country Between Us. *All the poems were about El Salvador, where Forché had gone as an international human rights worker. And it was she who in a way coined the term, "the poetry of witness." But it seemed that one had to go elsewhere to witness, because there was some feeling that, domestically, we had* nothing *to witness.*

GK: Yes. You search for your death threat somewhere abroad.

MB: *Yes, and I think that there is still something prurient about this. Just the other day, for example, I found myself saying to someone, with a certain degree of embarrassment, that I "wanted" to go to Auschwitz.*

GK: Go there, go there! I would suggest it to you, and to everyone. I was not there until '82, and I said "Why should I go there, I can imagine it?" However, it's good to go there, to touch those walls and to look at those shoes and to look at the hill of hair which is now completely gray, because it was once maybe black and blonde and brown, all kinds of hair. But it became gray, the whole stuff. It's good to be there. And to touch somehow the extremes, to touch the walls of the executions.

MB: *I agree with you and I plan to go, but there is always this feeling one has in these situations, this need driven, I think, partially by guilt, partially by the allure of the horrible. If we don't have it in our own lives, we go and seek it out, and then we write this literature of witness which often, somehow, still seems partially contrived. We know we can get on the plane at almost any minute, leave Beirut or El Salvador or Auschwitz, and be back home in the suburbs.*

GK: So we probably cannot win in every respect of our lives. We are all winners as well as losers. And what we win in social success and safety and sophistication, we will lose at the other end of the scale.

MB: *I often think of that childhood game where you have something like an air-pocket under a blanket, and you push it down in one place and it pops up in another, and you push it down again. Life often strikes me as very much like this—you push the problem down here, or you push the censorship down in one place, and it pops up somewhere else.*

GK: Yes, and I would say that people also *search* for their suffering; they find their own suffering, because there is probably a need to do so. You can experience total suffering from a divorce if you don't have any other reason to suffer.

MB: *And not necessarily a morally inferior suffering at that.*

GK: No, no, all types of sufferings are justified. But I personally don't believe that this need for suffering is not also a tendency towards self-pity, towards narcissistic self-pity. So it's not the purest stuff of human emotions. And there is also a type of passive suffering, of cowardly suffering: you give up and suffer instead of doing something. Because I am older, I'm a little bit bored with these constant complaints of the suffering. Survivors are not in such terrible despair, and I myself have never laughed so much as I have at self-dramatization, the telling of terrible stories. Because I feel that the terrible stories that I survived, although they can be very painful, are sometimes also terribly funny or grotesque or neutral or cold. You can have so many approaches to your own past.

MB: *It reminds me of a novel by one of my favorite poets, Howard Nemerov, called* Federico, The Mask of God, *in which one of the characters says, regarding something another character has told him, "Oh, how terribly sad." And then he pauses briefly and says, "And then again how very funny." In your own life, one of the things that interests me most is this whole question of optimism. You say—or, rather, your stand-in David Kobra says—"I owe my life to a series of fortunate coincidences." And clearly you were fortunate in many ways. There were 207 children in your village and five or something like that survived.*

GK: Jewish children.

MB: *Jewish children, yes. This question of being a survivor, which I can imagine must give you a very interestingly ambivalent attitude, because, on the one hand, you obviously witnessed so much suffering and tragedy, yet on the other hand you were a beneficiary of such great good fortune. And I think that, for a child in particular, the same suffering that is so awful for adults may seem almost—how else can I put it?—entertaining. I think of people who have told me stories of the bombs falling in London when they were children, and they said that it seemed to them, at times, like a spectacular kind of party, a fireworks display.*

GK: I had the same experience. For instance, we lived in a seven-story house during the siege of Budapest, and on the top floor was a terrace, a flat terrace, and we poured water onto it and it was a place where we could slide, even ice skate. And we did it, and in the meantime there were the Russian hunter planes—*ratas* they were called—and they shot at us. And, yes, it was interesting, the danger. And we didn't run away, we continued; somehow we lived with the danger. Whether it was funny, I don't know. Every day was a small victory that we were still alive. And of course it *was* funny when once a cannon shell came into the room where we were eating our bean soup. And parts of the window fell into the bean soup. Then we "fished" the glass pieces out of the soup, and it was somehow funny.

You know, once I had a circle of older friends, most of them are not alive any more. They had a funny name for themselves, *The Thousand Year Club,* because all together these people had spent a thousand years in prison. It was a bit exaggerated, but many of them spent many years. When they got together, you might imagine that it was a very sad company or evening or dinner. But no, it was full of laughter because they evoked the stories of their imprisonment, how one or the other was comical or ridiculous, and they laughed at each other and the evening was full of good stories. A little bit like the military years of elderly gentlemen. It's in this way that peasants are wise, because in this village where I now have a house, when somebody dies, everyone from the neighborhood, from the village, comes together. The women come together and prepare a great meal, and they drink and eat and are merry. And so it recreates the authority of the life.

DECEMBER 1992–MAY 1993

HERE'S TO THE HAPPY HUNGARIANS!

It's an old technique in the annals of the unhappy (ask any psychologist)—especially when armed with that great god of modern civilization, statistics—to project their unhappiness upon others, finding in this rather lugubrious project a redemptive sense of their own (comparative) happiness. Where Hungarians are concerned, the griefmongers are well-armed: there are more than enough statistics to go around. Suicide, alcoholism, divorce, heart disease—those four great indices (for those who specialize in such matters) of personal despondency—why, yes, the Hungarians, indeed, are international gold medalists in each of them.

Yet how do these somber statistics translate into daily life? I've often wondered about this since coming here. Do they *really* mean that Hungarians are a dark, self-destructive, pessimistic people, a race of *skototropic* (from the Greek, meaning "seeking out the darkness") scavengers madly in search of the next way to defeat and/or destroy themselves?

"We're so surprised," a couple of French friends who recently visited commented almost immediately upon arriving in Budapest. "We expected, from everything we'd heard, that the Hungarians would be walking around with their faces down, wearing dark brown and black, never smiling, all fat and depressive looking. But the people here seem very friendly, alive, sexy, animated."

"Yes," I said, "welcome to the spread of disinformation: just one more divergence between what's advertised and the actual product. It's the *Westerners* who, I suspect, beneath all their superficial friendliness and Club Med personalities, are more depressed than the Hungarians will ever be."

A bit of rhetorical exaggeration on my part, perhaps, for the Hungarians, given their history, do have some things to feel depressed anddispirited about (though also, given their lively and accomplished culture, much to celebrate). Yet, before leaving this lovely country and its people for the summer, I thought I might (like the good literary person and occasional psychotherapist that I am) offer alternative "interpretations" for some of these now-well-publicized categories, just by way of suggesting that it may not be the Hungarians, but rather ourselves, who might be counted among the truly somber. So, here goes:

1. **Drinking**: A traditional imbibing of the nectar of the gods, a willingness to participate in the Dionysian/Bacchic pleasures of life, to alter our constricted consciousness sufficiently to release us from some of its inhibitions.

2. **Heart attacks/poor diet**: An acknowledgment that not everything that gives pleasure in life (e. g., *kolbász, virsli,* goose fat, *túrós táska, gesztenyés kifli,* etc.) serves to enhance longevity; an unwillingness to sacrifice quality, as John Steinbeck once put it, "for a small gain in yardage."

3. **Divorce**: A living enactment of the rather fundamental, albeit uncomfortable, truth (confirmed by the sociobiologists) that the spending of one's entire adult life with the same person—while it may be highly consoling and, in many cases (especially for the rearing of children) advisable—is a largely unnatural act, hardly an adventure for the adventurous (rather, a triumph, as the writer Donald Barthelme once put it, of "the dull gravy of common sense" over "the hot meat of romance").

4. **Suicide**: An option which—for many spirits greater (though perhaps more troubled) than our own (e. g., Friedrich Nietzsche, Arthur Koestler, Primo Levi, József Attila)—can provide a certain consoling

possibility for acknowledging that life is no longer, or has never been, entirely what one had hoped for. At the very least, however, an acknowledgment of the fact that one had the courage of great expectations.

The truth is—though some of the above are intentional exaggerations intended for effect—I *haven't*, in my nearly a year here, found Hungarians to be a depressed, or depressing, people, but, rather, for the most part lively, musical, friendly, outgoing, sexy, energetic, intelligent, demanding, and subtle—not, perhaps, the most comedic people on the face of the earth, but certainly not islands of funereal pessimism and downward-sloping shoulders.

There is even, I would suggest, a possible "other" index of happiness—a questionnaire from which Hungarians would emerge at least as life-affirming as almost any other people I know—as follows:

1. How many times have you made love during the last month?

2. How often have you recently played an instrument or taken profound pleasure in listening to music?

3. How many times have you truly *enjoyed* (rather than inhaled) something you've eaten, drunk, touched, seen, read?

4. How many times have you walked around your city—or wherever it is you may live—and observed to yourself, "What a beautiful, romantic place!"?

5. How often have you felt a profound joy in the pleasures of your own language? How many times have you felt your tongue reverberate to a sound as lovely as the word *"Egészségedre"* ("Cheers" or "To your health")?

These questions, I realize, will never be asked by the statisticians of what currently passes for happiness or well-being. But their answers, I would suggest to you, may tell us more about true happiness and resiliency of spirit than divorce, suicide, or hardening of the arteries ever will…more, that is, about *un*hardened hearts, resilient spirits, a sensual and life-affirming view of the world. For music and lust and daily pleasures of all kinds, though they may say little about how long or disaster-free our lives will be, are certain indicators that, at least, we are truly alive…as, it seems to me, so many Hungarians, their faces raised proudly into the polluted air, are—citizens, not necessarily of a longer life, but perhaps a better one.

So—as I sign off for the summer to return to the land of the long-married, long-living, tofu-munching, Pepsi-imbibing ektomorphs (a species, it occurs to me, which would make a fine sequel to the Houhynyims and Brobdinagians)—I raise a glass of *Tokaj* and a *kolbász* in praise of the joyful, life-affirming *Magyars*.

And *"Egészségedre"* to you, too.

JUNE 1993

MAGDA:
A WEINSTOCK
AMONG THE LIVING

The moment I first lay eyes on her, across the room of her photo shop at #3 Madách utca, I know this is love, the kind only possible between a man and a woman, that instant attraction referred by the Jungians as the recognition of one's *anima* personified. I'm not certain if it's the gray hair and slightly saddened expression, which remind me of a photograph of my grandmother taken just before she left Nazi Germany in 1938. Or the richly veined, capable hands, the Old World-looking widowy black dress, the kindly, slightly whimsical eyes. But this, I immediately realize on entering the store, is not merely an encounter, but a kind of destiny. *This* is a woman I need to know.

Apparently, as is so often the good fortune of those struck by what is commonly known as "love at first sight," the feeling is mutual, for Magda looks up from the contact sheet she is examining so carefully with a magnifying glass, smiles, and asks me—as though sensing that we are, perhaps, connected from some previous life—if I speak German. I do, and now there's no stopping us. The fates, the fickle gods of love, will have their way. Like Romeo and Juliet staring at each other across the ballroom at the Capulets, we're destined to be.

It turns out, almost immediately, our sense of mutual recognition has a geographical dimension as well: Some sixty years ago, in the spring of 1933 to be precise, Magda Radó opened her first shop, the RADÓ MAGDA LAB, at #56 Damjanich utca, literally ten feet from where I now live, at #58. "I was born in 1906 in Nagyvárad, which is now part of Transylvania," she tells me. "After my mother died of stomach cancer, when I was eight, I stayed with my grandmother in the small village of Bethlen, which was the home of Bethlen István."

Magda's half-sister, a child of her father's first marriage, was already living and working in Budapest at the time. Her father, an expert watch-maker who had been trained in Switzerland, owned a small jewelry shop in their village. "Everything he did he did wonderfully," Magda recalls proudly. "He was even a fantastic billiards player. But," she adds somewhat sadly, "he also was quite a gambler, and it seems he gambled away everything we had in the billiards halls."

Magda's mother being already ill at the time, her father moved to Budapest to make a fresh start while Magda remained with her grand-parents in Bethlen until 1920 when, after the War and the Trianon Treaty severed Transylvania from Hungary, she left by wagon ("Not," she says, "at all like a Holocaust wagon. It was very comfortable.") for Budapest. The trip took a week, and, upon arriving in the capital, she continued to live in the wagon for the entire summer before moving into a Budapest apartment with her grandparents in the fall. Magda's sister, meanwhile, had moved to America, from where she wrote, "If only the climate were better here, it would really be God's country."

At the age of sixteen, Magda began studying photography in Budapest, an apprenticeship that lasted three years. After ten years working as a photographer, she married Péter Radó, a worker in a large paint-manufacturing plant whom she met at a dance school run by her brother's wife. When their two children—a boy, Tamás, and a girl, Mari—were born, the Radós, both of whom were Jews, converted to the Evan-gelical Lutheran Church.

"We converted for the children," Magda explains to me. "My hus-band said it would be safer for them. But in my heart and feelings," she adds, "I am a very good Jew. This anti-Semitism I see around me only *strengthens* my feelings of being Jewish.

"We thought of ourselves as *Hungarians*—of the Jewish religion, but Hungarians. We were patriotic citizens who were proud of our country.

Of Jewish religion, but of Hungarian nationality."

After her marriage, Magda worked at a large photolab named PHOTOLABOR until her husband helped her open her own shop in 1933 at #56 Damjanich utca, now the site of a small *söröző/étterem* where I often stop for an afternoon *palacsinta* and coffee. "I had a good name in the business, because we did such good work," says Magda. "Then the war came and I could no longer work. I couldn't photograph, but had to work in a large lab with many employees."

"Why?"

"Because I was Jewish."

"But I thought you had converted."

"Yes, but I stayed Jewish in feeling, and most people knew I was Jewish. I was lucky however. When they began deportations from the ghetto, I wasn't in the ghetto. We were hiding on Damjanich utca in a cellar, with the whole family, living illegally. We waited for the deportation, but they hadn't come for us yet."

"And others knew you were Jewish?"

"The whole neighborhood knew, everyone."

"And you still feel Jewish today?"

"Yes, 100%…in my feelings. I follow the Ten Commandments faithfully—they are my religion.

"Then, in November of 1944, a friend and I decided to leave Budapest. We went eighty-four kilometers by foot with the soldiers. The officers were very, very decent. They were Hungarian soldiers. It was often raining, the grass was wet, and we slept outside. My children had stayed with my mother-in-law in Budapest. My husband was on a work brigade, and I hadn't heard anything about him for half a year. But he was lucky; the commandants were nice to him, and he wasn't deported. But we didn't know where he was. And he didn't know where we were.

"We finally arrived at a small village where we decided to try and escape. It was nine o'clock at night. The officers were so decent they allowed the old and sick who couldn't carry their packs to leave, especially if they had some money. That night, we slept in the grass. There was a large marketplace. And in the morning we kept walking. It was then that we decided—my friend and I—to escape. One of the soldiers knew we were trying to escape, but he agreed to help us. We arrived at the village. The streets were completely empty. Finally, a car came by, with only a driver, an elegant Hungarian man. He stopped. I asked, 'Are you alone? Are you going to Budapest? Can my friend and I come with you?' He had a very slight accent. I asked, 'Are you Hungarian?' He said, 'No, I'm the chauffeur for the Swiss Consulate.'

"It was a miracle," Magda continues. "He asked if we had documents. I said no. I didn't want to lie. He then said, 'O.K. come with me to Budapest.' And he took us home to his housekeepers, who were Hungarian Swabians…very decent people."

"And what happened to those who had been left behind in Budapest?" I ask.

"The next day, the Arrow Cross came and took them away. If I had stayed one day longer, I wouldn't be here now. They took all the older women…not one of them came back.

"The next day, I went back into my lab on Damjanich utca, and we stayed hidden there with my in-laws. I had hidden some supplies there, and we had gas, water and electricity, so that we could live there.

"I too could have gotten an affidavit from Wallenberg," she continues, "or could have gone to America, since my sister was living in New York, but it seemed stupid to me. Just because my sister was living in New York, why should I be entitled to special treatment? Wonderful

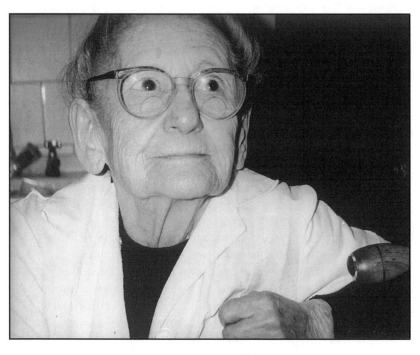

Magda Radó, nee Weinstock, at her Radó Photo Lab,
Imre Madách ter, Budapest, January 1997.

times, those were. We hunted for bread like dogs. We didn't have any food coupons, since we had to remain in the ghetto...hidden on Damjanich utca."

"Did you know what was going on in the death camps?"

"We heard some rumors, but we didn't know anything for certain."

"And what about anti-Semitism in Hungary today? Do you think there is any?"

"Very, very much."

"How can you tell?"

"People don't know that I'm Jewish now, and I hear them talking."

After the war, under the Communist Rákosi regime, Magda had to go to work in a communal photolab and close her shop, since she could no longer get papers for a private enterprise. "We were forced to do this," she says, "since people were supposed to work together communally."

After several years, a new law was passed allowing her to privatize again, and, thanks to her husband (who was working for the government at the time), she acquired her present store, at #3 Madách utca, where she has worked with her daughter Mari for the past fourteen years. ("Do you live together as well?" I ask. "No," they say, almost in unison, "God forbid.")

Magda's only son (Tamás), a judge, died at age 48 of Parkinson's disease. Her husband (Pál) died at age 78 in 1984 after fifty years of marriage. "This work keeps me alive," she says, gesturing around her studio. "I leave my house in the Zugló every morning at 8:00, take the tram to the metro, and then the #1 bus. Since I lost my husband, this keeps me going, that I can come here every day and work."

During the '56 Revolution, of which she has boxes of photographs stored in the photographic treasure-trove that is her store, Magda kept coming to work every day as well. She kept a box in her store to collect money to help families affected by the Revolution.

"Every family's story is a novel," Magda says to me, and it's the novelist within me (I not long ago published my first novel, *Weinstock Among the Dying*, the name of whose protagonist, Martin Weinstock, came to me for no apparent reason)—as well, perhaps, as the man in love—that can't, for some mysterious reason, resist asking Magda one last question.

"By the way," I say, curious but unsuspecting, "what was your family name before you got married."

"Weinstock," she says. "Magda Weinstock...why do you ask?"

JULY 1994

77

LOOKING FOR "ÁRPI BÁCSI"

It is not part of the common socio-political vernacular to refer to a nation's president as "cute," yet he is (at least to those who like to think of human beings in such terms) cute. It is not part of ordinary discourse to refer to him as "sweet," yet he seems—not like saccharin, but more like clover honey—sweet. One does not ordinarily refer to one's political leader, however duly elected, as "uncle," yet here in Hungary he, the nation's most popular politician, is *Árpi bácsi*—"Uncle Árpi," everyone's wise old uncle who became, miraculously enough, the nation's first democratically elected president. And he is, strikingly, a man who seems like he might be more comfortable in the company of those he has translated (Faulkner, Hemingway, Styron, Updike and Doctorow) than in the corridors of power, as if to testify to (or, perhaps, call into question) Emerson's famous paraphrase of God's edict that one can have power or joy, but not both.

I had, in fact, been looking for *Árpi bácsi,* in a sense, since first coming to Hungary, as any writer arriving in, say, the Czech Republic might be looking for Havel—out of a curious blend of envy and curiosity towards a writer who has left his desk (or, as is the case with many Central/Eastern European writers, his prison cell) and ascended the podium, the writer who has, so to speak, traded the printed page for the political stage, the audience of his soulmates for one, more expansively, of his countrymen.

"How may we recognize him—that contemporary of mine, somehow over sixty—the nameless Hungarian?" Árpád Göncz the writer, as if gazing into a mirror, asks in his introduction to his *Homecoming and Other Stories* (Corvina, 1991). "This Hungarian will automatically have lost six years of his life which he owed the devil, and will carry the marks of the two deep creases at the corners of his mouth."

And so I, too, recognize him—this small man dressed in a black suit and thin red tie, this man with the knowing, whimsical smile who seems untouched by the aura of power that now surrounds him—as he walks into the crowded room at ELTE, the university where I serve as a visiting professor. He appears somehow smaller yet larger than all those around him, here to attend the opening of the WORDPLAY exhibit jointly sponsored by The British Council and ELTE's School of English and American Studies. For, in his person as well as in his fiction and plays, *Árpi bácsi* is a man endowed with the hard-won humility that allows him, like all great men and women touched by a history not of their own making, to remain subservient to, rather than seek to dominate, the materials of his life.

"As a president with limited powers," he said, speaking more like a poet than a politician in an address to the September Academy Intellectual Forum in Vienna in November of 1993 (and echoing sentiments expressed by Václav Havel on accepting the German Peace Prize several years ago), "I am daily made aware of the moral weight and social force of the *word*. Of the *articulated word,* which is my tool and daily bread."

And Göncz's "nameless Hungarian"—the man who "has marched twelve hundred miles through an endless succession of battles on frozen feet," whose "home and his land were taken from him, his place of work was nationalized," who "found himself in a forced labor camp, or in prison, and when he was let out had to start his life all over again and harbor his 'soul' in a deep inner immigration," the man who fought in the struggles of the '56 Revolution and its aftermath and whose face "carries the scars of this struggle, too, like some peculiar badge"—is, of course, in large measure Göncz himself.

The Hungarian president served the six years he "owed the devil" after a closed, secret trial in which, together with István Bibó (with Imre Nagy, one of the major political martyrs of the failed Revolution), he was sentenced to life imprisonment for his role in the uprising. It was during those six prison years that he learned English, a fact for which, he writes, "if nothing else, my confinement was worthwhile."

Yet Göncz—whom his friend and fellow writer, George Konrád respectfully refuses to call anything but "Árpád" ("'Árpi,'" he says, "sounds too much like a brainless old uncle for a man of such depth and intelligence") still speaks English hesitantly, almost shyly, like a man too humbled by what he doesn't know perfectly to display it. So that when I, only half-timidly, approach him (for why be timid approaching your uncle?) and introduce myself, he shakes my hand warmly and turns momentarily away from his conversation with the British Ambassador. I explain that I had come to know him first through his stories, rather than his politics, a fact he seems to appreciate so deeply (and, in part, wistfully) that I am reminded of Shelley's description of poets as "the unacknowledged legislators" of their times. I then tell him how, as an American, I find it strange—indeed, a tad alarming—to be able simply to walk up to him at a cocktail party in a room devoid of bodyguards, Secret Service agents, and security measures. (I'm well aware that my own President was at the time scheduled to arrive in Budapest in just days accompanied by an armada of such.) "Ours," he says with a noticeable, but partly elegiac, sense of gratitude, "is still a small, intimate country. We are not yet in need of such protections."

The next night, in fact, I see Göncz again—this time at an evening of readings and conversation at the Radnóti Miklós Színház in honor of the literary quarterly HOLMI's fifth anniversary. He is seated, inconspicuously but for the diffused reflection of stage lights off his mostly bald head, in the third row, beside HOLMI's literary editor Sándor Radnóti. In that posture, he seems to be as he belongs and feels most at home—just another "nameless Hungarian" among his literary countrymen, the kind of man you would like to have for an uncle, or—should you be among the truly blessed—for a president as well.

FEBRUARY 1995

GOD BLESS THE MAN
WHO'S GOT HIS OWN

Life is unfair.

JIMMY CARTER

The bartender at the Captain Cook Pub down the block from my writing studio—a svelte, very attractive Hungarian girl of nineteen by the name of Brigitta with Caribbean-like magenta-colored skin, has a boyfriend who's older than she is—more than twice as old, in fact, weighing in at a ripe young forty-seven—a Hungarian rock drummer by the name of Lajos. As I pass her on the street 'most every morning— en route, *not* to reading Simone de Beauvoir, but to the solarium—it is hardly the resigned air of the victim or the harassed that she exudes. In fact, I've seen her and Lajos together on numbers of occasions, and—in the course of my closet career as a semi-official anthropologist in the realms of the happily and not-so-happily intertwined—they are hardly, from either vantage point, one of those couples who arouses my pity.

WHEN HISTORY ENTERS THE HOUSE

About a year ago, on a brief tour of Southwestern Transdanubia, my wife, son and I, and a couple of American friends, stopping at one of Hungary's many converted castle/hotels to spend the night, were introduced to our host, a rather hefty, forty-eight-year-old former Budapestian by the name of László who, after a *pálinka* or two in the hotel bar, explained to us—sheepishly at first, but, as the conversation progressed, with obvious pride and pleasure—that the young girl behind the hotel desk, just about to enter into her third decade, was not, as we had initially supposed, his daughter (or a local high-school girl earning some extra cash), but his girlfriend. "I'm not quite sure what she sees in me," he confessed later in cracked German, "but we're very happy together."

Among our best friends here in Hungary are a rather well-known writer, a man nearly twenty years past my own age, his third wife, whom I'll call Zsuzsa, a baby-faced, fleshy girl of a mere forty (the same age as my own wife), and—along with their two young boys—their young daughter Rózsi—young enough, assuming everyone along the generational ladder got an early enough start, to be her father's great-granddaughter. They, too, hardly appear, to the innocent, or not-so-innocent, observer's eye, to suffer from afflictions not equally well-dispersed upon the population of the similarly aged.

I remember as I write this a conversation with a certain middle-aged Lebanese man in a Washington, D. C., café some years ago, in the course of which he informed me that—in his country, at least—it was considered rather extraordinary, if not perverse, for a man *not* to marry a woman at least twenty years younger than he was, a fact which, if true, would suggest that a sexual harassment attorney in Lebanon, were such a species to exist there, would probably make Johnnie Cochran look like a pauper.

The world, of course—especially the world of the politically correct and morally cleansed—is chock full of rhetoric espousing the evils of such unions—most of it, I can't help but having noticed, voiced by those with a deeply personal stake in their seemingly abstract ruminations (either women who have been, or fear being, dumped for younger women, or men without the gumption, or attractiveness—but hardly ever without the desire—to find them). As for myself—married to a woman whose forty years provide me with an impeccable moral shield against such accusations—I, along with most of the men I know in ideologically more "correct" marriages, would be a damned liar if I didn't confess to the fact that more than a mere twinge of envy passes through me when I see a man my age seemingly reborn in the company of a woman half his own.

Some twenty or so years ago, in fact, that same point was very aptly, and humorously, made in the movie "The Four Seasons," in which, among four couples who were very close friends, one of the men (played, I believe, by the politically unblemished Alan Alda) dumps his equal-aged wife for a much younger woman. To the other couples' unrelenting chagrin, he brings his new partner on their joint vacations, but now he prefers loud, grunt-filled, below-deck sexual acrobatics to the quieter diversions of on-deck martinis—an effort at relaxation which his morally purer same-age friends, for lack of a more convincing passion, continue to engage in, eating their hearts out all the way.

That, behind such age-diversified unions, there often lurks the not-all-that-happy story (see Newt Gingrich) of a heartlessly dumped wife or, worse yet, neglected children, there is little doubt. Life, as Jimmy Carter well knows, is largely an unfair business, and, for every man who can keep his desires locked in the safe deposit box of his heart, there are, I have no doubt, hundreds of others for whom it more than occasionally seeps, like it or not, into their bodies. And, for those who like the scales of their justice perfectly balanced, there always remains the consoling possibility that—when the older man's prostate begins to go, his hair to whiten, his glands to clog with something less arousing than semen—his still-marketable lovely companion will find a more promising happiness (as one of mine once did) in the arms of some testosterone-infused young hunk on the ski slopes of Aspen or Telluride, conscience be damned.

"Pleasure," a hardly self-denying friend of mine once said, "is the only justice," and, though there are those who would (rightfully) argue with such a one-dimensional view of the matter, there are far worse formulations for what one person can give to another. For myself, at least, whether or not I stay married to my largely same-aged wife and keep watching the spectacle from my safe front-row seat, one thing these imperfectly balanced, two-tiered couples do for me is to remind me that *nothing*—no matter how much we would like, or, in our ardor, *demand* for it to be otherwise—will cure life of life itself, that even what, for lack of a better name, we call *love* is not so much a hedge against life's injustices as a reflection of them.

MAY 1995

PART IV

THE ALLURE OF EXILE

A. A.:
THE EXTRATERRITORIAL

The most basic premises of life in Eastern Europe, observed Polish poet and critic Stanislaw Baranczak in a 1984 essay entitled "E. E. [Eastern European]: The Extraterritorial," are so different from those of America as to constitute almost a problem of translation. Though much has changed in Eastern Europe in the almost ten years since Baranczak's observation, you still need to spend only a few months here in Hungary to discover, on going back, an almost endless list of things about your now-former country that may serve to shock you. First, there's the space. Even Boston—nestled snugly in America's most densely populated Northeast corridor—resembles, on first glance, an off-season Yosemite: *Where have all the people gone?* The stores—cavernous corridors of emptiness between an unconscionable variety of brightly colored items—seem as spacious and underpopulated as the ski trails of Aspen at 6:00 A.M. The jogging tracks?—Why, they're empty. And *this* is the so-called "fitness explosion"?

And what about the roads? Suddenly seeming more like runways than streets (this moving in a car without having my teeth jolted by potholes and mislaid cobblestones at every inch: Could this possibly be *driving?*), they cry out for automobiles to use them. If this be "traffic," I say to myself, driving through Cambridge at rush hour, then what must barrenness be? My rented Ford—practically noiseless, seemingly inert for its failure to spew forth clouds of thick black exhaust, its brakes so silent and well-oiled that squeezing them feels more like kissing—could it *really* be a car? Is the relationship of this vehicle to the Lada, the Trabant, the Wartburg not at least as remote as that of *homo sapiens* to *Australopithecus?*

And the colors (as Baranczak has observed): What sort of world is this, not utterly dominated by browns and grays? This orgy of purple turtlenecks and yellow tights? This day-glo heaven of smiles and superficial greetings? And these zealously friendly people in the checkout line—Why in God's name are they introducing themselves? And who in his right mind *cares* who's sitting next to him on a the bus? And why are all these people sitting down in the first place? Don't they realize this is no way to be prepared to flee—as Eastern Europeans think they always must—in the event of a sudden invasion or revolution?

And the newspapers: So thick—how could anyone possibly want to read them? My body sags with the sheer weight of the *Sunday Boston Globe* (nine-tenths of which, I realize upon arriving back home, consists of advertising and other "news" I wouldn't read even if I were stranded on Philoctetes' Lemnos). And the girls: So blond, so soapy-smelling, so seemingly—at one and the same time—flirtatious and sexless. Where have all the lust and evil gone (long time passing)? If I felt like a kind of American grouch before, it's a funeral director I feel like now: My cheeks threaten to crack with forced cheerfulness. And this coffee in paper cups—how could anyone possibly want to drink it? (An hour in a so-called "café"—cramped tables, coffee that tastes like dishwater, a waitress who brings the bill while I'm still stirring—costs me as much as two full days of eating and imbibing along the Danube.)

As in my "past" life, I make lists on yellow legal pads: Any *one* of my fifteen errands would require the better part of a day, if not weeks, in Budapest. (One of them, in fact— *"have computer fixed"*—would take months...and more than twenty times the monthly income of the average Hungarian!) But with all this unimpeded efficiency in my daily rounds, why is it that I suddenly feel so nervous? Why doesn't this breezing through the various maintenance activities of my day make me—oh God, here goes that terribly American word again—"happier"? But then again, there's the language: Not a single word consisting of a string of *t*'s, *z*'s and *c*'s strung together by *s*'s in sight! What pronouncorial bliss!

ALLURE OF EXILE

I go to Washington, D. C. , walk the halls of Bill Clinton's Transition Team: These people, too, why are they so cheerful? Have they no sense of what they are about to embark on? Of the mess they are about to inherit? These denim-clad, nearly hysterical-with-smiles portraits of Bill and Al staring out at me—could I possibly imagine József Antall or Árpád Göncz in a similar pose? Or Václav Havel?

And the subways! So empty you could bring your bowling ball, so clean (in D. C. at least) you're tempted to eat off the floor. So what if, during my brief week in our nation's capital, a young woman is murdered ten feet from my door? This, after all, is America, the land of opportunity (even for murderers).

1. Barbara Walters
2. Wonder Bread
3. Stand-up parties
4. Baseball

are some things American which Baranczak says E. E. will never be able to come to terms with. To which list I'd add—as the Authentic American (A. A.) returned for a visit:

1. Oprah Winfrey
2. The low social standing of prostitutes
3. The color purple (*and* the book!)
4. "Creative Writing"
5. "Date rape"
6. Coffee "to go"

to name merely a handful.

"Should we have stayed home and thought of here?" the poet Elizabeth Bishop asked in her poem, "Questions of Travel," and I have sometimes asked myself as well since returning to Budapest from that place where "home" used to be. But, in the meantime, Thomas Wolfe was wrong: You *can* go home again—only you'll find it stranger than ever, emptier, bigger, smooth as a runway taking off for God-only-knows-where.

DECEMBER 1992

91

THE GIANT WHO GOES
PART-WAY WITH ME

Having often traveled, but never lived, abroad, I have spent much of my adult life wondering about, and at least partially believing, the truth of Ralph Waldo Emerson's oft-quoted sentiment that "my giant goes with me wherever I go." Knowing, after all, that we carry our psychological selves, despite our best (or worst) intentions, into any situation, the allures of such escape from self and history that geographical change seems to promise always seemed to me dubious at best. I once remotely knew someone (a friend's son) who, feeling quite suicidal in America, decided to "escape"—*à la* Hemingway, typewriter in hand—to Spain, only to discover that a change of venue was, indeed, not a change of fate: He, sadly, changed only the location, but not the nature, of his demise, committing suicide there.

But now, living some 5,000 miles from home—not even in the Europe with which, by birth and marriage, I am relatively familiar, but in that "other" Europe, so strange and unfamiliar—I find that although, surely, my giant is still here with me, he is somehow smaller, freer, a bit less of a burden constantly riding the back of my daily life. Living in a new place, one has, to be sure, a past; but it is, for the most part, entirely a past of one's own, known by no one you don't want to share it with, held against you by no one you don't arm with its knowledge. Whatever your youthful follies (or virtues) may have been, they no longer, in the person of others, confront you daily: The lover you may have treated badly just a year ago is now safely ensconced in some distant Santa Fe, some unincriminating Hawaii. If you've been a liar in your past life, you are now, until proved otherwise, a harbinger of truth. Your resumé, at least for the moment, is of your own making, or your own re-making. A known-to-be-married man in Denver, you are now (until proven otherwise, with whatever advantages or disadvantages you wish to make of it) as solitary and available a soul as ever haunted the cafés of Budapest, a man with only a present and a future, and a past entirely yours for the inventing (or re-inventing).

Of course, there are the seemingly etched-in-stone, unalterable elements of personality itself: Reticent and suspicious in Fort Lauderdale, you are likely to be the same in Madrid, though your lack of intimacy with the language may allow you to escape detection as merely "shy" or "intimidated." He who was an incorrigible flirt in Toledo is no less likely to keep his eyes on his driving on the busy streets of Budapest, and at least as likely to get into an accident while he peruses the local distractions. But that same accident, a catastrophe in Boston, proves to be merely a minor inconvenience, another piece of on-site anthropological fieldwork, in Hungary.

So there's a freedom in all this I didn't expect to relish. Looking over my shoulders (as those who live in places like my usual home, Cambridge, are prone to do), I see not yet another Nobel Prize-winner, but only the unknown and imaginable faces of Hungarian strangers. Crossing the streets in mid-afternoon, I need not confront yet another re-crimination-filled stare of a student to whom I gave a "B" some four years ago out of the sheer hardness of my heart; or the angry gaze of yet another writer whose reading I failed to attend, whose most recent book is still waiting for my praise. It is not so much that, walking these streets, I am a man without a past, as that I am a man who *fully owns* his past…and who is free, for the moment, to invent a new one.

Literature, of course, is replete with characters who, hoping to find a new self in a different venue, found to their discouragement that not only can't you go home again, but you can't even, very successfully, go away. Yet, thinking about it now, as I turn from the corner of this café and smile at yet another beautiful woman who knows nothing about me, I would not nearly as readily dismiss as I once did the sentiments of the airline passenger who, more years ago than I now care to remember, turned to me from the window seat of a 747 about to land in a place where he had no history, smiled, and said, with a breath of relief, "Isn't it great to be someplace else?"

Maybe it is.

FEBRUARY 1993

SO MANY BORDERS,
SO LITTLE INTEREST

O Europe is so many borders…

József Attila, "O Europe"

One of the reasons I fell in love with my wife, some years ago in Quito, Ecuador, was because of the (to me) lovely and charming way she, in her inimitable French accent, pronounced the words *statue quo*. I've always loved accents and differences, which—given the fact of having been an American child growing up in a German-speaking home adjacent to a Spanish-speaking neighborhood, now a man married to a French woman, living in a Hungarian city with a son attending an all-Hungarian-speaking kindergarten—is, no doubt, a fortunate proclivity, a proclivity, in fact, which may have led me to *choose* some of the aforementioned "coincidences" to begin with.

So that, living here now in Eastern Europe, where borders—both those that are obvious and those that aren't, both those which already exist and those which are rapidly breaking down into yet more and more borders—are rampant and often anything but salubrious, I'm all the more troubled when, as I did recently, I see a headline reading "America's Many Accents Fight the Ancient Battle of Bias" (*International Herald Tribune,* March 3, 1993), describing the situation in my own supposedly borderless country. In the article, among other vignettes, a Columbia immigrant recounts her embarrassment at pronouncing her own husband's name "Yoseph," the kind of embarrassment which would long ago have driven my own wife—not to mention my parents—into hiding, if not exile. And I, too, wonder as I make my way through the Pestian streets, leaving a wake of mispronounced *jó napot kívánoks,* *viszontlátásra*s and *én amerikai vagyok*s behind me—am I, now, the object of ridicule and embarrassment because of my Americanaccent? Should I hurry off to sign up at the "Accent Reduction Clinic" that, no doubt, some zealous young American M. B. A. with a good nose for profit has already founded to save us foreigners from the terrible humiliation of being—God forbid!—somehow "other"?

But accents, of course, have traditionally been emblems of culture, and cultures always emblems of difference, and—as I turn to survey a world in which Serbs and Croats are shedding one another's blood, Flemish Belgians and Wallonian Belgians hurling epithets and worse across their non-existent border, Irish Protestants leaving bomb-containing vehicles parked on Irish Catholic streets, Slavs and Czechs surveying the wreckage of their recent divorce, and more—I can only think of the words of Lithuanian poet Tomas Venclova that "the whole value of world culture resides in its variety of traditions and languages; but when language and ancestry turn into an amulet for saving one's life in time of slaughter, I would rather be the one being slaughtered."

Have we, I wonder as I survey the havoc and carnage which my fellow man is currently wreaking upon my fellow man, reached that point in world history where language and culture are little more than "amulets" for one group's ascendancy over another, mere rationalizations used to justify our innately prejudiced and bloodthirsty natures? Is even the more-or-less monolingual American "melting pot" we pride ourselves on having created little more than a homogenizing stew that can no longer tolerate anyone (with the possible exception of Arnold Schwarzenegger) who doesn't sound as bland and character-deprived as Dan Rather?

Yet still there are, as George Konrád so eloquently reminds us, "some enlightened citizens who do not loathe their fellow men just because they are what they are...[who] do not feel any inclination to declare themselves refugees. Some few minority groups of this passionate description also try to do something in order that their city should become interested in rather than wary of the different." For difference, as Konrád so well knows, is what makes a city cosmopolitan rather than provincial, a melting pot rather than a festering cauldron.

One small thing we can do, it seems to me, is to wear our accents proudly, to remind ourselves—in the words of a New York City public school teacher who emigrated from Columbia over twenty years ago—that "when you have an accent it gives you a certain originality, something that is singular, something that is yours." We could, perhaps, *use* our accents—and the accents of others—to remind ourselves that, bigotry and intolerance (and borders!) notwithstanding—the sum of a world filled with genuine individuals might yet make a whole. And *that,* friends, might be a *statue quo* well worth hanging onto.

SEPTEMBER 1993

THE ALLURE OF EXILE

The streets are dirtier than my own, the air so filthy from spewed congestion of Trabants and Ladas that a blackish veneer of soot forms nightly on the sills of our windows. The life expectancy (for men) is a good fifteen years shorter than in the U. S., testified to most recently by the death, in recent weeks, of no fewer than three acquaintances who had not yet arrived at even my own forty-five years. A successfully completed (local) phone call seems almost a triumph, the language is replete with to-me-unpronounceable *cs*'s and *sz*'s, the diet more frequently soaked in lard and goose fat than life-affirming tofu and margarine. So why remain in exile in this *goulash*-laden once-Communist backwater when the calm, ecologically sounder, politically correct shores of my own country still beckon so clearly?

"It could indeed be said," writes Eva Hoffman in her beautiful memoir *Lost in Translation,* "that exile is the archetypal condition of contemporary lives," and, given the experience of most contemporary, postmodern lives, one would be hard-pressed to disagree. Cross-cultural marriages, international jobs, borders and walls erected and torn down by New World Orders and by rekindled old ones, the world seems, ironically enough, more and more a single community and less and less home to anyone. Indeed, the word "home" itself seems to have become one great abstraction—"the place," as Robert Frost once famously put it, "where, when you have to go there, they have to take you in." But as to the question of who *they* actually might *be,* the great bard, safely ensconced on his New England farm in a world which no longer seems to exist, remained mute.

"I am most jealous," writes Hoffman, echoing my own sentiments, "of those who, in America, have had a sense of place." And yet I remember, in Cambridge some years ago, the writer Thomas McGuane's reaction when I remarked that I—coming from an immigrant background, growing up without English as a first language, being married to yet another foreigner—thought of him enviously as a "real" American, safely grounded on his Montana ranch, at home in the native vernacular and landscape. "There *are,*" he answered, "no real Americans. *No one* feels at home here."

Indeed, it seems we (or, at least, terribly many of us) have all become metaphorical gypsies in a world without borders, but also without security. "A sense of belonging and of natural inheritance," writes Hoffman, "is what I long for"; and who doesn't? Yet she, as if in response to the unanswerability of her own longings, has recently moved to England from the States, to which she, in turn, was "exiled" as a thirteen-year-old girl from Cracow.

And why, I now ask myself after two years of "exile" in Hungary, not go home—back to my own bastion of freedom and opportunity, where friends speak my language, there's always a dial tone when I pick up the phone, the cars all have catalytic converters, the health food store's just down the block, and the funerals are mostly for the old? Why not, now, go home and *think* of here?

Warnings, after all, abound concerning the dangers of exile, especially of the voluntary kind. "Transplanting yourself into the soil of a foreign language," writes Polish poet and scholar Stranislaw Barnanczak (himself now in exile in Massachusetts), "makes you, as a rule, wilt rather than flourish, feel deprived rather than enriched. In our human Tower of Babel…identity may ultimately come down to what is lost in translation."

But there is—I have come to realize during my self-created, and still extending, exile—also something to be gained from that condition. "I don't want a city," writes George Konrád, "where what I detest is a duty and what I love is immoral, where everyone tries to educate everyone else…where if I love one human being I cannot love another, and my body, if it desires another body, must feign shame; where I can find joy only in what I own—my son, my dog, my mendacious pictures... where the ground plan of apartments teaches us to hate one another."

I, too, don't want such a city—don't want a city where a man looking at a woman, or teaching her, or bumping into her at a Xerox machine lives in perpetual dread of being accused of sexual harassment; where all forms of honest discourse and feeling are politically incorrect. I don't want a city where my son's schoolmates are almost as likely to carry knives as books, where I am more likely to die at the point of a gun than from an excess of sausages, where nothing that money can't buy seems worth having and the president's past sex life gets more media attention than his present efforts to reform health care.

Here, in exile, my son goes to daycare for $10 a month, I can lounge over a single twenty-cent cup of (good) coffee for hours without being terrorized by an (in turn) terrorized waitperson, a woman can still be (dare I say it?) *sexy* and attractive without feeling objectified, a man desirous without being a vulture. (Eye contact between the sexes, in other words, is not yet the exclusive domain of litigants.) Here in exile I'm still asked more frequently about what I think than about how much I make (euphemistically: *"What do you do?"*); friendship is still a value having less to do with equivalencies of power than mutualities of passion; politicians still look (and seem) more like recent graduates from ordinary life than from the Kennedy School of Government's Summer Seminar or Grecian Formula 9 commercials; and lovers still smooch in the streets, Puritans be damned.

In exile, the semi-permeable membrane with which one is forced, on one's native soil, to surround oneself merely to screen out the superfluous grows more permeable: One hungers, in fact, for the humble twenty-six weekly pages of the English-language *Budapest Sun*; one greedily strains to overhear a few scarce whispers in one's native language in a café in the midst of the Babylonian cacophony of so many tongues.

In addition, there are fewer of us here—we're bigger fish in a smaller, but happier, pond. I've found an ex-Harvard professor (or mere human being) to be happier in the cafés of Budapest than a present-day one on the streets of Cambridge. (Competition, while it may be good for the national economy, has never been found to be a balm for the nerves.) And the luxury of a bi-national self, rather than indicating a pathological schizophrenia, may merely tear down the walls impeding a New World Order from within. "What from one perspective appears a split personality," writes Baranczak,

may turn out to be a profoundly advanta-
geous "multivalent consciousness"; the gap
between the two languages may become "a
chink, a window, through which I can observe the diversity of the world." The
immigrant's "Babel syndrome," may be just
another name for the ultimate recognition
of the human world's maddening yet mag-
nificent plurality.

Exile, of course, can merely become a form of aggravated homeless-
ness, a salt rubbed into the wound of our ongoing sense of alienationand
displacement. Or, it may, on the other hand, prove to be a kind of balm—
if not a healing, then at least a reprieve; if not a solution, then perhaps
a more interesting way of addressing the question, of coming to terms
with our own sense of foreignness and *internal* exile. "If I become aware
that I am somehow myself part of this foreignness," writes Hungarian
essayist and philosopher László Földényi,

that this universal otherness not only
touches me, but has been latent in me from
the start, then I discover the common de-
nominator of the political, existential, psychological, ethnological or religious meaning of foreignness, in which they resemble
not only one another but myself. I then learn
to live with this foreignness, for ultimately I
wish not to filter out of my life everything
which, measured against myself, is foreign
by emphasizing my own identity, but to find
through the acceptance of foreignness the
way to the foreignness within myself, back
to the long-ignored, persisting, forgotten
root of my identity.

It may be, taking Földényi's argument to its logical conclusion, that
one can, ironically enough, feel oneself more in exile at home, and
more at home in exile. And if, as Hoffman suggests, we are all in exile
anyway, why not, I ask myself, opt for the real thing?

MAY 1994

ON FEELING
LIKE A CENTRAL EUROPEAN

For anything unready, yet
ready too, I lie in the sun:
let the redeeming nowhere come.

GYÖRGY PETRI
"DAYDREAMS" *(ÁBRÁND)*

"We longed for the ordinary unhappinesses," Nadezhda Mandelstam wrote, mainly because the ordinary unhappinesses seemed, by comparison, such a luxury. But lyrical line though it may be (for example, a wonderful epigraph for a poem!), the thought itself misses a certain fundamental truth about all unhappinesses, ordinary *and* extraordinary: Allowed to enter deeply, to reverberate within the very psyche and soul of their recipient, they're all, more or less, alike—those who've received them, the walking wounded and betrayed, all straggle about with more or less the same kind of limp. No matter how history may have entered the house—in the guise of a Russian tank, in the uniform of an Arrow Cross soldier, through a death in the family, or via a broken childhood love—all false pieties be damned: It affects you equally.

In America, for the most part, unhappinesses—ordinary and extraordinary—aren't supposed to hurt, or, at the very least, are supposed to find their elixir in twelve steps of some "anonymous" nature, preferably in a rented church hall. Ultimately, we're all supposed to chin up and, whether we want to or not, "have a nice day" (which, of course, misses yet another psychological mark—namely, that one man's nice day is the next's Inferno).

"People who need people," Barbra Streisand tells us, "are the luckiest people in the world." But the experience of most Central/Eastern Europeans says precisely the opposite: If you need other people too much, you may well be screwed...and not the way it feels best. The Jews of this region needed other people most, and their decimated numbers, their crumbling, abandoned synagogues, poignantly tell the story of where that particular need got them. All over Central/Eastern Europe, the ghosts of "people who need people" are still walking about, limping into an afternoon *söröző,* having another *pálinka,* hiding behind a new name or a story too painful to tell. In the steamy, mid-afternoon waters of some cathedral-like *fürdő,* they rest their aching bones in the hopefully healing waters and cry out, "Checkmate!"

Here in Central Europe, it's still all right—in fact, quite normal— to be melancholic and sad. Too much good cheer, in fact, is still considered (as I consider it) a sure sign of a dim wit and a spray-shot intelligence, in whose spray most things of real truth and significance, for better or worse, are lost. Here, you can still say to a woman, raggedy or beautiful, *kezét csókolom* ("I kiss your hand") without being slapped with either a sexual harassment suit or just plain slapped. (The war between men and women is still the same old war, punctuated, gratefully, by momentary cease-fires.) You can even, if you're lucky and nervy enough, simply walk up to a beautiful woman on the street and say, in cracked Hungarian, "Hey, baby, you're gorgeous, wanna _____?" and, if you're truly among the politically incorrect and the blessed, it may even happen.

Pepsi, of course, has now made it here, quick on the heels of Coke, and, wherever it goes, can the "Pepsi Generation," with their aerobicized bodies and love-of-life smiles, possibly be far behind? But, for the moment at least, it's still all right to be a moody and melancholic, woman-loving sybarite here—a man more preoccupied with sex and death than with that newer kind of sex and death disguised (poorly) as life: making a quick buck.

"Once upon a time there was a town, then a village, then a megalopolis, and then just Hell," might well be a quick history of our times (or, another way of putting it: "The wall fell...but it fell on us."), the only hope for redemption from which is that, within the megalopolis, there may still be places where the village is alive. In Budapest, at least, if you're lucky and eagle-eyed enough, you might still be able to slip into the courtyard of a building on Király or Wesselényi utca and find some old codger who'll fix your antique fountain pen or your sixty-year-old Continental typewriter...or, at the very least, sell you a new (old) one that actually works.

Some years ago, on a ski lift in Vermont with a former student ofmine, I was blown away (in the ordinary sense) when—on what was no more than a five-minute excursion with a man neither of us would ever see again—she took off her goggles and gloves, turned to the stranger seated between us (the lift, alas, sat three), and made—in her squeaky, American voice—a series of introductions memorable only for the utter waste of time and energy they entailed. Like so many Americans, she reminded me of Basil Hallward's immortal words to Lord Henry in Oscar Wilde's *The Picture of Dorian Gray:* "You don't understand what friendship is, Harry," he says, "or what enmity is for, for that matter. You like everyone; that is to say, you're indifferent to everyone." In Central Europe, on the other hand, where everyone knows even your best friends may inform on or betray you (or, at least, stand idly by while you're carted off to Majdanek or Bergen-Belsen), such wastes of one's limited reservoirs of charm on a perfect stranger seem utterly unecological, thank the Lord.

Perhaps—having grown up among the scarred, the lame, the surviving, the ill, and the aged—I'm more accustomed to, and more comfortable with, this slowed-up pace of conviviality (resulting, predictably, in far deeper intimacies). A certain grumpiness and reserve, I've found, rather suits me, as does a certain deep contentment...the kind, for example, you can find being grumpy and reserved with a kindred grumpy and reserved spirit. Everyone is wounded in the end, the conventional wisdom seems to say here, so why not sit back, grumpily, and enjoy it?

"Hell is other people," said Sartre, that mousy little Frenchman (who might have been a Central European himself) in love with sex and death, and if it is, why not enjoy it? A good shot of *pálinka,* a beautiful, politically incorrect ass draped only in a G-string, a fine slab of high-cholesterol goose fat, and a frown as wide as Lake Balaton and you're ready to go. And as for "Have a nice day"? Well, you can have it.

JULY 1995

PART V

IN SEARCH OF
A CENTRAL EUROPEAN METAPHOR

IN PRAISE OF BATTERED CITIES

For the first time I recognized the truth of beauty: that it is brokenness, it is on its knees.... I could sit, merely breathing, and be part of it. I was beautiful—at last. And I didn't care—at last. I stumbled through the ancient streets, stopped in the smoke-grimed coffeehouses and added my signature of ash, anonymous, and yet entirely satisfied.... I was, simply, in the most beautiful place I have ever seen, and it was grimy and sad and broken....

PATRICIA HAMPL
A ROMANTIC EDUCATION

The city Hampl—in her eloquent, lyrical memoir—is speaking of is Prague. But, for me, it is Budapest—beautiful, battered, grimy, ever-"improving" Budapest, city of chipped paint and shell-pocked walls,

Danubian jewel of such a multiplicity of browns and grays that the two colors themselves have taken on rainbow-like dimensions in my imagination, city of prostitutes and drunks, of polyester-clad entrepreneurs and self-made millionaires in imported clothes, city of recycled gravies and exhaust-spewing Ladas and Trabants, city of politicians who look like children and poets still undomesticated by universities, city of *Túró Rudis* and grime-caked stained-glass windows, city of sybaritic baths where the odors of urine and sulfur and the commingled juices of lovers and curative minerals inhabit the air, city of wet kisses on bridges, in tunnels, on esplanades and park benches, city of *kréms* and *túrós táskas* and *pálinkas* and *somlói galuskas*, city of jeweled boats and floating casinos and stationary brothels, city of peep shows and sex shops and *húsbolts* and *dohánybolts,* city of dilapidated merry-go-rounds and puppet theatres, where *az élet nem habostorta* ("life is not a piece of cream cake") and everyone knows it, city of pilfered treasures and drunken security guards, city of crumbling buildings that sometimes (alas) collapse in the first light of morning, city of odd juxtapositions of condoms and bananas and oil filters exhibited in a single store window, city of overpriced blue jeans, city of Konráds and Petris, city of Esterházys and Árpáds and Gönczes, city of unpronounceable drugstores, which, *lassan, de biztosan* ("slowly but surely"), I have come to love—How do I love thee? Let me count the ways:

What do you love so much about Budapest? they always ask. *Isn't it, well, a bit primitive?* Yes, friends, it is a bit primitive, a bit sad, a bit tragic, a bit unfinished, a bit tainted, a bit melancholic—yes, yes, the way the beautiful always is and always has been tainted, primitive, slightly sad, unfinished, tragic, eternally hopeful. What is beautiful here—what has stolen my heart the way not even a beautiful woman has ever stolen my heart (now, finally, I realize why so often, in literature, the allure of a city is equated with the allure of a woman)—is precisely this: its grimy lifefulness; its beautiful, pock-marked facades; its tattered dresses; its slightly musty, lived-in scent of usage and pleasure; its dark underbelly; its lardy women of *jó hús* (lovely meat) and its slightly unshaven, nicotine-stained men; its deeply sad, beautiful melodies of wistfulness and longing; its resonances of Bartók and Kodály, of Liszt and Ferenczi, of the sad, youthful suicide of József Attila and the graceful, autumnal one of Arthur Koestler.

In Budapest the future beckons to us with hope precisely because it is not yet realized, not yet perfected. Like a small scar on the underbelly of an otherwise perfect creature, it perpetually cries out to us

A Central European Metaphor

human! human! in its palpable griminess, its discrete lack of urgency and subculture of stolen pleasures, its ebullient inefficiency. Here—as one of the city's great celebrators, George Konrád, puts it—"entire streets are bulletin boards...all visible matter is sculpture." Held up to us like the mirrored conundrum of our complexities and desires, the city reflects both the shabby and the glorious vicissitudes life holds in store for us. Like a cat, it is passionate and tender, at times penurious, at times generous with its affections, but exactly as it chooses: It refuses, defiantly, to submit to our ever-domesticating wishes.

If a city, as Lawrence Durrell once wrote, becomes a world when one loves just *one* of its inhabitants, Budapest—a city whose allures, whose charms, whose brazen sensuality flatly resist the claims of such a singular fidelity—suggests to us the somewhat romantic, though deeply revivifying, possibility that, if we can love even one human being (or, by extension, one bridge, one monument, one gorgeously dilapidated building), we can surely love another.

In Budapest, above all, the dead are allowed to cohabit peacefully and vitally with the living, continuing to circulate among us in their tarnished monuments, their periodically recycled and resurrected street names, their grimy, often partially shattered, stained glass windows, their perpetually revised and embellished personal histories. Unwilling to release us from the grip of their sad music, they free us from both false modesty and shame, from that excess of morality and good cheer that freezes the face into a false smile and the body into a false conformity of right behavior. So that—whenever a dark sense of sobriety or doomed fate threatens to overtake me—I readily head for the nearest *söröző* and follow the advice of a certain Hungarian writer I know: "Refuse modesty, drink to every life in this jewel of a city that you made yours."

MARCH 1994

113

BOSTON-TO-BUDAPEST DIARY: IN PRAISE OF ANARCHY

> I wanted to cut through this resisting struc-
> ture that let loose an ever-growing traffic on
> the overburdened town center, and build a
> new city in its place, in whose identical
> neighborhoods families, equal in social po-
> sition, would no longer disdainfully keep
> apart. I was going to move vehicular traffic
> underground, break up the airless corridors
> of the streets, rehabilitate and turn into an
> uncrushable king the pedestrian.
>
> GEORGE KONRÁD
> *THE CITY BUILDER*

The narrator of George Konrád's beautifully written novel, an archi-
tect in an unnamed Central European city, is far more sophisticated

than the above quote might suggest: His vision, like a great city itself, is multi-dimensional, ironic, highly textured. It is a vision capable of entertaining "witty and mostly unorthodox solutions to tricky tasks," a vision that knows that—in the life of a city as in the life of individuals—"there are as many moralities as there are relationships."

Perhaps no "relationship" more intimately acquaints one with a city's texture, with the local nuances of the relationship between *cosmos* and *polis,* than that with one's car (or lack of it). The car, for better or worse, has become, as the feet once were, modern citizenry's chief means of navigating its world, so that the places where, in any particular city, we can or can't put it (and the penalties for the latter) say a great deal about the kinds of choices that city has made.

Take Boston for example—a city where owning (and, ergo, parking) a car is roughly akin to waving a Palestinian flag at a B'nai B'rith convention. To own a car in Boston or Cambridge—and to attempt to park it for more than five minutes in anything but your privately owned (or leased) parking space—is to invite the collective wrath of the Puritan bureaucracy (in the form of the police department, towing companies, and a veritable army of meter maids) to descend upon you with a speed sufficient to make the fall of the guillotine seem like slow motion. On more occasions than I care to remember, I've left my car, engine running, in front of, say, a dry cleaner's for all of thirty seconds, only to emerge to find a $15 ticket flapping in the breeze beneath my windshield wipers.

The bright side of all this, I suppose, is that a certain kind of blessed order pervades the Boston parking scene: A car parked within field goal distance of a crosswalk—not to mention helter-skelter on sidewalks, grassy embankments, in front of driveways and halfway into the intersection, *à la* Budapest—is likely to involve its owner in an all-night chase that will end up at Tommy's Towing somewhere in Dorchester (many miles from the original *loci dilecti*), at a cost that could purchase a night in the bridal suite here at the luxurious Gellért. But the streets, meanwhile (*grâce à* somebody's *Dieu,* but not mine) are a soporific pedestrian's, and a certain kind of urban planner's, idea of Heaven.

So that—environmentalist though I am intellectually—a sense of blissed entitlement, of enraptured permissiveness, infused my whole being when I first arrived in our blessedly chaotic *Magyar* capital. *What peaches and penumbras!* as Allen Ginsberg once wrote. What heavenly chaos! Slapdash, slovenly angled, protruding, extruding, exuding, and eluding (the authorities), my Honda (and—here's the rub—its catalytic converter!) could suddenly be left everywhere...anywhere. Just think: An entire city as your parking space, sidewalks and all! I was ecstatic, like a man who, with a sense of complete calm, had left his brand new Rolls Royce in front of the World Trade Towers (before the bombing) and gone off to spend a month on Mikonos.

But now, according to the Budapest City Council, our lives are about to be "improved" (a word I have come to associate, in the twin worlds of politics and urban policy, with a diminution in their quality). Bureaucracy—in the form of a new super-agency to deal with Budapest's enormous parking "problem"—will come to our rescue. Regulated and supervised (for our own good, of course), we will be permitted to graduate from the (admittedly) ambiguous blessings of automotive chaos to the tedium of bureaucratized order. Budapest—that city to whose sensuous disorder I once (1986) fled from the Hapsburg fastidiousness of Vienna—will, I fear in my darkest moments, exchange a violent disorder for the subtler violences of a tediously exacted order.

Do I prefer, you ask, the choking, lead- and carbon monoxide-drenched air of Ladas, Wartburgs, Trabants and diesels? Armadas of cars parked so close to buildings and storefronts an underfed ballerina would have trouble squeezing her way between them? Of course not—for my young son's sake if not my own. To be perfectly candid, I'd prefer a city—a truly *human* city—in whose downtown *no* cars, with the exception of delivery trucks and taxis, were allowed, *period*. But *"Sauber,"* we must remember, in the words of George Konrád again (translated into German from the Hungarian), *"ist kein Synonym von bunt"* ("Clean is hardly a synonym for colorful"). Nor is "safe" necessarily a synonym for "life-giving." Or "regulated" for "animated."

So that some of us—all the risks and inconveniences notwithstanding, and until the aforementioned Nirvana comes to pass—may still prefer to see a small flotilla of Ladas angled chaotically along Vörösmarty utca (as they are this very moment) than a platoon of *kaahs,* as they say in Boston, *paahked* ever-so-obediently *in Haahvad Yaahd*...yawn yawn yawn.

MARCH 1993

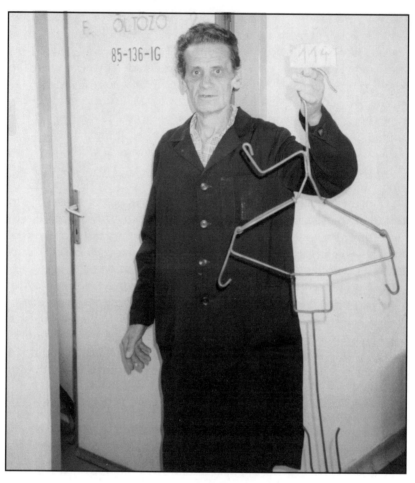

Josi-băcsi, the swimming pool men's locker room attendant accompanied by the infamous hanger, at Eőtvős Loránd University, Budapest, January 1997.

IN SEARCH OF
A CENTRAL EUROPEAN METAPHOR:
THE HANGER

Its image has haunted me ever since I first laid eyes on it in the locker room of the university swimming pool in Budapest during the summer of 1992. It was as if I knew from the beginning there was something at once beautiful and metaphorical about its unwieldiness, something so perfectly resonant latent in its imbalance and cumbersomeness that it would become, or already was, a kind of metaphor for my life in Hungary, if not for Central Europe itself. Alien at first (at least to one weaned on the immaculate cleanliness and functional efficiency of Washington, D. C.'s National Capital YMCA), seemingly impenetrable in all its usages, so oddly imbalanced and (to every appearance) unbalance-able, it sat there like the misshapen third-grader who had once sat in the first row at everyone's elementary school, considered, one day, a genius by the rest of the class, the next a freak.How could I possibly hang my things on it? Where would the shoes go? The pants? How was even the remotest possibility of achieving an equilibrium on its disheveled, bent, jaggedly hooked torso conceivable? Where to begin?—The underwear? The jacket? The shirt? The shoes? Like some cast-iron, Cold War Albania, excluding from its borders every potential visitor, it beckoned, yet warned: *Stay out.* What to possibly place in its misshapen center? A rolled up magazine? A crumpled scarf? A foil-wrapped sandwich?

Like an animal tamer, I circled this odd creature, trying to see it from all angles, exchanging gazes, wanting to penetrate its mystery. A condemned prisoner—in my worst imaginings, an inmate of a death camp— the cold, metallic gaze of its number stared back at me, reproachful and accusatory as a sculpture by Joseph Beuys...or, at the very least, one of his misshapen suits. Was this, I thought to myself, the Central European analogue of Warhol's Campbell's Soup cans? The physical embodiment of the Polish joke once so prevalent in America? ("How many Hungarians," such a joke might begin here, "does it take to learn how to use a hanger?") Was the square-shaped, pubically located center, I wondered, a male masturbatory relic from the days before the inflatable sex-shop doll? An antiquated noose? Was the entire object, perhaps, a recycled instrument of torture once employed by the secret police in the basement labyrinths of #60 Andrássy út? (The various hooks, I imagined, gouging out the eyes and/or disfiguring the body, as in a Jerzy Kosinski novel.)

I circled and stared, thrust and parried. I gingerly placed my shirt over the left-handed eyelet hook. (The hanger, I soon realized to my amazement, comes in the left-handed and right-handed variety.) Like a beleaguered scale, a slightly punch-drunk boxer, my adversary swung wildly to the right. In search of an equilibrium, I countered, placing my underpants on the middle right hook. The hanger, like a minutely calibrated compass, tilted slightly leftwards. I then attempted to drape my pants, like a piece of cloth ballast, over the bent center bar, only to have my wallet, keys and *bérlet* (metro pass) fall to the floor. Perplexed, I hung my trousers like a shroud over the hanger's hooked and numbered face, which merely triggered a sharp tilt to the right once again.

My boots, I thought. *My boots will help balance this all out. My boots are the key to victory over this dumb animal.* I forced the two elongated, upward-curving bottom hooks up into the toes of my boots. Like the last gasps of a defeated bull, the hanger heaved cumbersomely from side to side for a moment before coming to rest. Then my boots, top-heavy against the thin hooks, fell to the floor. The hanger swung wildly again, coming to rest at about a sixty-degree angle to the floor.

Ah-hah, I thought to myself, *I know what I'll try next: I'll move my pants to a lower hook, thus lowering the center of gravity as well. As they say at the gambling tables of Las Vegas, I'll raise the ante once more.* My pants (a new pair of 3,000-*forint* beige trousers from Kleider Bauer) merely swept the locker room floor from that position, becoming cuffed in a sooty gray. Unwilling to admit defeat, I again considered my Hungarian-made boots (courtesy of a crowded *cipőbolt* on Teréz körút) once more from a distance, realizing the leather eyelets on the rear might have been designed with just such a challenge in mind. Guiding them, one in each hand, gingerly towards the hanger's lower extremities, I watched as—incredibly—they glided with the ease of a young skater at Városliget park onto the metal stirrups and—*voila!*—with what seemed a groan of resignation like a pinned wrestler's, the hanger took a deep breath, straightened, and hung, limp as a beached whale, at a 180-degree angle from the metal bar.

There remained, however, the challenge of my coat. Where on the beast's back could my coat possibly go without either disturbing thetentative equilibrium I had so painstakingly created, or causing one of the hanger's ominously curled appendages to pierce like a fisherman's hook through the jowls of its expensive, French-made leather? Still fresh from the victory of my boots, my underwear, and my socks now dangling from the mis-aligned side hooks, I was in no mood to start from the beginning. I had, after all, come for a swim, not a fight.

Like an outmatched child who, bleeding from the lip, runs home to his mother, I decided, just this once, to take the easy way out: What good, after all, was there in a Pyrrhic victory whose only tangible result would be a small moral triumph and a wasted afternoon? Swallowing my pride, I knocked on the *öltöző* door and summoned my gap-toothed friend Josi-bácsi, the locker-room attendant, to my side. With a good-natured *"kedves barátom,"* he draped my jacket like a misshapen scarecrow over No. ll4's neck, straightened the collar, and zipped it up. The hanger, sensing some small victory of its own, seemed to smile, tilting slightly again to the side.

I smiled too. My small boat, as Elizabeth Bishop writes in her poem "The Fish," filled with victory. Now there was no turning back. Soon I would even be able to make a Hungarian phone call without reaching the wrong party, have a pair of *fött virsli* (boiled sausages) for breakfast without wincing. I was beginning to feel at home in Eastern Europe. The days of exile were drawing to a close.

JUNE 1994

WAITING FOR BREAD
IN HEGYMAGAS

How simple and frugal a thing is happiness:
a glass of wine, a roast chestnut, a wretched
little brazier, the sound of the sea....

NIKOS KAZANTZAKIS
ZORBA THE GREEK

We begin to gather early on Saturday morning—at about 6:45, in fact—I and the various *nénis* and *bácsis* (mostly *nénis*—a good portion of the *bácsis* having gone the way of most Hungarian men past sixty) of Hegymagas, a small non-touristic village some five kilometers from Lake Balaton, eagerly waiting in front of the town's only *vegyesbolt* (grocery store) for the arrival of the bread truck from the "big city" of Tapolca.

Even the town's most conspicuous drunk—a slope-shouldered fellow of about thirty-five who, were I a casting director, I would assign the role of Mellors, the gardener in D. H. Lawrence's *Lady Chatterley's Lover,* and who spends most of the rest of every summer's day seated in a semi-stupor at one of the wooden tables in front of the *italbolt*—is there, as if to suggest that, in Hegymagas's hierarchy of gustatory values, bread still supersedes both *pálinka* and wine (though it may be, it occurs to me later, he is merely waiting to see if any good-looking girls get off the bus that is soon to arrive—well ahead of the bread truck—from Tapolca as well.)

Vera *néni,* our landlady—dressed in archetypal widow's black to acknowledge her husband's recent death (a fringe benefit of which, I indelicately remark to my wife, is that it forced her to change out of her off-putting pungent gray garment of the previous summer)—is there, too, as is the elderly gentleman I greeted, carting his rake and pitchfork out to the field in a wheelbarrow, on the dirt road leading from our wine-maker's house just minutes earlier, who now explains to me—in rusty, countrified French—that he spent four years in North Africa with the French Foreign Legion in the 1950s.

Promptly at 6:58, the first of the store's two proprietesses arrives, unlocking the front door and bringing the refrigerated leftovers of yesterday's dairy products (there is, I notice, no leftover butter) and *virsli* (sausages) in from the storage area around back. Ten minutes later, the bread truck's still not in sight, and the words *nincs kenyér* ("no bread") are beginning to reverberate, like an air-raid warning signal, through the town, a full half of whose population is now lined up outside. A few young children, dressed in their Sunday best (though it's Saturday) and bearing flowers of various sorts, are making their way to the bus stop, no doubt to visit their various *nagymamas* and *nénis* in Szigliget and Tapolca, and—as the word of our delayed *kenyér* spreads—the patch of street between the *vegyesbolt* and the *zöldség-gyümölcs* (fruit-and-vegetable) stand across the street more and more resembles a kind of feminized *boules terrain* in the South of France.

At about 7:15—in the one car on the street that is *not* a Trabant but rather a well-polished blue Opel with a conspicuous "D" stuck to its rear bumper—the town's unapologetically German couple (both sporting expensive watches and clinging for dear life to their pocketbook and wallet) arrive in search of their *Frühstücksbrot,* offering up a decidedly non-Hungarian *"guten Morgen"* as they enter the store; then, after leaning against their vehicle for another five minutes in hope of salvation, decide to enact the old adage that God helps those who help themselves by driving off to Tapolca to pick up their bread personally.

A Central European Metaphor

Those of us who remain—most of the others exchanging various bits of local gossip; I, with (as the former French Foreign Legionnaire tactfully points out to me) my fly wide open, trying with limited success to expand my Hungarian vocabulary—have begun, no doubt, in the eyes of the casual passer-by to resemble a kind of early-morning street fair, united by our joint enthusiasm for the still non-existent *friss kenyér*. An occasional widow drops out of the competition by entrusting her 58 *forints* and plastic shopping bag to a neighbor, another succumbs to the call of more significant duties (gardens to tend, *pogácsa* to bake, cherries to pick) by settling for *fél tegnapi kenyér* (a half loaf of yesterday's bread) or deciding to return later. Among those remaining, some wait outside, eyeing the curve of Route 84 for signs of the *kenyér*-Messiah, while others jockey prematurely for position in front of the *vegyesbolt*'s archaic cash register.

By now, various remedial suggestions (call up the baker in Tapolca, send a personal envoy, etc.) are reverberating through the cherry-scented Hegymagas air, until, finally—at right around 7:30, the baker's tardiness on the verge of erupting into a major news story—the younger of the store's two female proprietors comes out to inform us that she has, in fact, called the baker, who has been delayed by some sort of "technical difficulties" and won't be arriving until the God-forsaken hour of *fél kilenc* (8:30).

What's a person to do? For my wife, Frencher than Charles de Gaulle, a breakfast without fresh bread and (non-rancid) butter is like, for the typical Hungarian male, a morning without *pálinka*. But this, I remind myself, is Hegymagas, not Paris. Not even the Internet will save us here. Vera *néni*, ever the realist, urges me toward compromise: *"Van tegnapi kenyér,"* she smiles through her gold teeth ("They have yesterday's bread"). And, of course, she's right—the price of such beautiful simplicity, of such a happily wasted hour, may be yesterday's bread. Which—at least in this writer's view—still tastes a helluva lot better than tomorrow's technology.

JUNE 1995

TEACHING IN HUNGARY: BEATING THE BEATEN SYSTEM

> Beating the system makes no sense in a
> democracy.
>
> GEORGE KONRÁD
> "BEING A CITIZEN"
> (WORDS TO SIGNERS OF THE DEMOCRATIC
> CHARTER, BUDAPEST, 19 DECEMBER 1991)

A funny thing happened to me on my way to becoming a Central European academic: I became a subversive. Let me explain:

You are an American university professor, coming, at least in all likelihood, from an institution where, insofar as the relations between faculty and students are concerned, certain things may be more or less taken for granted: I. e., (1) that the students will come to class; (2) that they will, while there, observe certain aspects of decorum and civility (e. g., not carry on animated conversations with each other while the

professor is speaking); (3) that they will, for the most part, do the as-
signed reading; (4) that they will (again, for the most part) neither rampantly plagiarize, turn in papers they have already handed in for other
courses, or engage in other forms of cheating.

In a nation such as America where universities are respected and
respectable institutions; where university professors are respected and
reasonably well-paid professionals; where university buildings and classrooms, for the most part, are "clean, well-lighted places"; where a university education (even in the humanities!) still seems to hold forth some
reasonable possibility, both intellectually and professionally, of having
a "pay-off," these assumptions still seem possible and true—metaphors,
in their somewhat domesticated civility, for the widely shared assumption that universities are respectable places with reasonable goals and
expectations more or less shared by those who (be they faculty, students, or administrators) occupy them.

But here in Hungary—a nation and people which I have come to
love and respect—as well as elsewhere in Central/Eastern Europe, both
the history and the current penumbral assumptions that go with it are
rather different. And, therefore, so is the experience. "Here," as one of
my former students so honestly and eloquently put it, "we were trained
to subvert, and prided ourselves on subverting, the system. The more
we cheated, cut corners, didn't attend classes, copied papers, stole exams, etc., the more we, and our fellow students and friends, felt we
were doing something respectable—we were beating the system that
was beating us."

But behavior learned under an unhappy system, like that learned
during an unhappy childhood, has a way of lingering well after the
particulars that summoned it forth have died away. (A once-beaten dog
continues to cower and whimper in the home of its new and benevo-
lent master.) And so—though socialism may be gone, though there may
be more and more professors (some foreign, many Hungarian) eager
and willing to care, more and more available and uncensored books
ripe for the studying—the old ways die hard: A professor (like this one)—
once accustomed to a classroom full of well-prepared, intellectually
curious, verbally demonstrative (not merely to each other), ethically
(sometimes *too*) well-indoctrinated young men and women—may now,
quite often, be presented with a class replete with rarely attending (un-
less threatened), largely unprepared, wildly gossiping (yet silent as stone
when *asked* to speak), rabidly plagiarizing young men and women.

In addition, such factors as starvation pay for academics (leading most of them to have two or three "other" jobs); infrastructural nightmares (insufficient and badly equipped classrooms, lack of office space, archaic machinery, non-functioning telephones); lack of university-wide communication (the left hand—often located at considerable physical distance from the right—rarely knowing what its counterpart is doing); and general lack of the comfortably bourgeois trappings of most American universities hardly help to instill that atmosphere of self-respect and significance of purpose that makes American universities if not the epitome of at least a reasonably comfortable stepping-stone to "real life." Though hardly, if ever, the cure for all ills, it seems clear to me that, insofar as the Hungarian university system goes, a substantial infusion of that classic capitalist lubricant—money—along with the creation of now-absent genuinely rewarding and remunerative professional opportunities in the humanities and other intellectual disciplines (cures which the present government seems unwilling, and unable, to administer) would go a long way in at least beginning to alter some of the aforementioned behavior.

Do all Hungarian university students cut classes, fail to pay attention, plagiarize papers, cheat on exams, and stare dumbly into space when called upon in class? Of course not. There are a large number of Hungarians students who—miraculously enough, given the present realities—attend class regularly, pay attention (even, occasionally, participate), write original and well-researched papers, and don't cheat on exams. Hungary's proud and accomplished heritage of intellectual achievement (far disproportionate to this nation's relatively meager population and the expectations that might arise from the linguistic loneliness of its language)—boasting figures as diverse as Bartók, Lukács, Ferenczi, Liszt, Kodály, Konrád, Szász, Radnóti, and legions of others—attests to that fact. Yet there is no doubt that the general, lingering atmosphere of subversion that permeates many Hungarian (and, I imagine, other Central European) universities exacts—on both students *and* professors—its toll.

Nor, of course, is this kind of behavior reserved only for the offspring of socialist cultures, or due entirely to this region's political history. My wife—a French citizen who was once a chiropractic student in California—readily confesses that, among the sizable group of French students attending her chiropractic college—cheating was considered not so much a grounds for shame as a badge of honor, an "imported" by-product of a French sensibility which, much like that of Central/Eastern Europe under socialism, might be paraphrased (in the words of yet another misbehaving Frenchman) something like, *"Je subverts, donc je suis."*

In addition, of course, there is alive and well here the age-old, highly traditional (East *and* West) European view of the professor as someone who fulfills to a "T" William James' definition of a teacher: Someone who must talk (without dialogue) for fifty minutes. Yet the occupational and intellectual hazard of such monologuing academics is that they may well find themselves neatly realizing yet another Jamesian definition of their professional class: *The natural enemies of their own subjects.* For the lively dialogue, the mutually informing and transforming intellectual exchange that is at the heart of American-style small-group teaching at its best, cannot take place when it becomes an almost universal consensus that there is only one person in the room worth listening to...and who must therefore (not the severest of punishments for many academics!) listen only to him/herself.

And what, we might now speculate, happens to the *professor* when confronted with such a to-him radically changed culture? For a while, of course, he goes on stubbornly (and, perhaps even, somewhat successfully) with his old, ingrained ways—preparing hard for class (e. g., doing his "homework"), trying his damnedest to stimulate and provoke discussion, introducing new materials, politely asking students to refrain from chattering to each other (or chewing loudly) while he is speaking, taking attendance, patiently listening to stories of unmissable ski trips, sick relatives, overly busy schedules, conflicting appointments, etc., etc., until, perhaps, his own psychotherapeutically nurtured sense of patience has been exhausted. He goes on, in other words, being who he was under that other not-necessary-to-undermine system, hoping that, like an aging George Foreman in the late rounds, he will eventually have taken enough of his younger opponent's body blows and lightning jabs to tire out the young chap and, ultimately, to score a knockout blow of his own, youth and resilience be damned.

But then, of course, there is the other possibility—one I have become increasingly aware of during this, my third year as a Visiting Fulbright Professor here in Hungary: The professor himself may decide—in defeat or fatigue or, perhaps, in mere compliance with the prevailing culture—to become subversive: He may begin to prepare just (at first) a little less rigorously, then even less; may start to repeat himself (a general occupational hazard for academics) even more than he once used to; may himself begin plagiarizing—in other words, "borrowing" lectures from colleagues or other scholarly works; may, in fact, start cutting class himself to attend yet another conference, go on (hell, if *they* can do it, why can't he?) yet another unscheduled vacation.

Very few of the above are things I, in fact, *have* done during my three years of teaching here in Hungary—but I would be lying if I didn't confess to having at least been tempted...and that some similar, if less radical, elements have at least sneaked "subliminally" into the ethical contructs that once supported my teaching. It was, as usual, a poet who put it best:

> Those to whom evil is done
> Do evil in return.
> (W. H. Auden, "September 1, 1939")

But what happens when, as here, the once-easily and proudly subverted system is no longer present? When, as George Konrád so aptly put it, "beating the system makes no sense"? When the victim of a subversion which was once a lifeline to selfhood and authenticity becomes the self itself—its intellectual and professional future, its survival in a "new" system which may no longer require (beyond what *any* system requires) a moral equivalence between subversion and survival?

These questions, it suddenly occurs to me, are ones I might well put to my own students this Thursday when—on what well may be my last day as a now slightly subversive Hungarian professor—I take them (in the good old "informal" American tradition) to Leroy's Country Pub for a drink...hoping, my fingers crossed, that most of them will actually be there, that we can make all our voices heard above the din, that—having collaboratively conspired to beat the already-beaten system (and having been somewhat defeated by the new one)—it won't turn out that we have too badly beaten ourselves.

MAY 1995

GOD BLESS YOU, MRS. KOVÁCS!

> The beginning of reform is not so much
> to equalize property as to train the noble sort
> of natures not to desire more, and to pre-
> vent the lower from getting more.
>
> ARISTOTLE
> *NICHOMACHEAN ETHICS*

BRAND LOYALTY FRUSTRATES reads the headline on Page 1 of the May 25th edition of *The Budapest Sun*, revealing a bit of Central European psychic inertia of near-cosmic proportions: **"Shoppers not swayed by fancy packages."**

To be successful in Hungary, the article quotes a certain Mr. János Tóth of the Hungarian Chapter of the International Advertising Association, "advertisers must fuel consumer desires by increasing product awareness," an enterprise whose high ideals are apparently wasted on a certain Mrs. Tibor Kovács, one of the still-unconverted heathens, who seems singularly unimpressed by the slick, Western packaging that has slowly made its way into Hungarian supermarkets. Mrs. Kovács, it seems, is a certain kind of neo-Neanderthal who prefers to stay with her tried-and-true (and much cheaper) Hungarian brands.

"How can three toothpaste commercials all say they are the best?" the inert Mrs. Kovács wonders, evincing a bit of folksy wisdom that might make all the Harvard- and Yale-educated scions of Madison Avenue (and Rákóczi út) wince with envy. "Hungarians just don't like the average advertisement," chimes in the fatalistic-sounding Péter Komlósi, international director of the public opinion research agency Szonda Ipsos. There is even a bit of near-psychobabble, provided courtesy of a certain Jim Williams, director of strategy and research at the London office of Young & Rubicam. "What I think will change in the next five years," he predicts, "is that people will begin to develop lasting relationships." *With what?* Why, of course—"With brands," concludes the psychologically sophisticated Mr. Williams.

Where once it was history—often (we should remind ourselves) a rather dark and unpleasant history—that entered the house of many Hungarians when there was a knock on the door, today it is (as it was just the other morning at my very door) more likely the man distributing free samples of Tix EXTRA, lemon fresh, a NEW detergent (brought to us, of course, by Procter & Gamble, Budapest) which proudly proclaims "better cleaning and freshness." And *that,* we might also remind ourselves, is a kind of less sensational, but equally revolutionary, history as well.

As in every society, here in Hungary too there are those who would employ change for high purposes, and those who merely wish to exploit it for low ones—those who wish to encourage the nobler human aspirations that usually accompany freedom (i. e., intellectual curiosity, professional opportunity, the desire for individual expression) and those who merely hope to exploit the baser appetites (i. e., greed, boredom, rampant consumerism) that are also inevitably unleashed in its wake.

Not that I wish to make the simplistically nostalgic argument that all advertising—or, for that matter, all the new or "improved" products it wishes to promote—is, *per se,* a matter of mere hype. The fact that there is, indeed, room for improvement (and, on occasion, genuine improvement itself) in the contents and choices being offered to Hungarian consumers —choices such as phosphate-free detergents or lower-fat dairy products, for example—seems to me one of the possibly genuine gains that might be available in this "Brave New World."

A CENTRAL EUROPEAN METAPHOR

Yet "wisdom," as William James said, "is learning what to overlook," and it may well be that learning to overlook advertising that merely seeks to promote false hungers (and *real* profits!), hype that arouses without informing, hungers that bloat without nourishing, *that,* in the present Central European context, may be wisdom as well.

And it may be that the intransigent Mrs. Kovács, rather than being yet another roadblock in the path to the great Hungarian future, is merely possessed of the wisdom of what the American poet Gary Snyder called "The Old Ways"—someone who may be wiser, even, than the present U. S. Vice-President Albert Gore who, mistakenly thinking something called the Information Highway is the road to the future, doesn't quite realize that it may just as likely be the road to hell.

So—from this writer, at least—God bless you, Mrs. Kovács!, as I and my equally intransigent expatriate family continue to brush with the same old (Hungarian) *AMODENT* toothpaste, shave with the same old (Hungarian) *CAOLA/BARBON* shaving cream, wash our clothes (apologies to Procter & Gamble) with the same old *MINNA tökéletes mosóhatás*, and breakfast on the same old (flavored with carrot purée!) locally produced *CERBONA* cereal, trying not so much to undo Young & Rubicam as to reassure our soul-mate Mrs. Kovács that, though she may not be riding the wave of the future, she deserves not to drown all alone in the waters of the still-useful past.

MAY 1995

PART VI

BRAVE NEW WORLD

THIS PRIVATE(IZED) LIFE

It being a good thing for ideologists, myself included, to be confronted now and then with the humbling reality of the facts, I thought I would pay a visit to my formerly favorite Budapest café, *Confectioner Művész*, recently closed for over a month due to "technical difficulties" (a euphemism for privatization), just to see what the new gods of private enterprise (in such close proximity to Budapest's fast-food corridor of McDonald's, Burger King, Kentucky Fried Chicken, and Pizza Hut) had now wrought.

When the *Művész* first closed in December, I, a kind of knee-jerk socialist at heart (an easy luxury for Westerners here, I remind myself, we having—to paraphrase the novelist George Konrád—the abstractions, while the locals have the ulcers), feared the worst when it re-opened: higher prices, uglier décor, a clientele restricted to Reebok-wearers. "No more poets in the sad cafés," as I wrote in an elegiac poem elsewhere. The rumors prior to the closing had, indeed, been rampant, my favorite being that those in charge of privatization had planned to level the *Művész* and replace it with a car dealership, only to have the well-known Hungarian short story writer, Iván Mándy, who has been known to frequent the *Művész* every weekday for years (he is, in fact, seated among a group of middle-aged and older men in the corner as I write), threaten suicide if the café wasn't retained in its present condition.

There were, of course, things wrong with the *Művész*, even in its previously "untainted" socialist incarnation. The hours, for one (10:00 a.m. to 8:00 p.m.) were a café writer's undoing, writers being notoriously creatures of either early morning or late night, the Muse a goddess who seems to loathe midday. Then there were the menus—more or less the traditional variety of the now-upscale *Gerbeaud* chain: difficult to decipher, tri-lingually confusing, modeled after the traditional seducer's art—i. e., offering more than the patron could actually deliver.

So now I'm here at the *Művész*—replete with clearly typographed green menus labeled *Művész Kávéház* and—*voila!*—reasonable prices. It's only 9:00 a.m., the glass-enclosed counter facing the door is replete with more *tortas, galuskas,* and *réteses* than any sensualist might desire, and etched into the large front window are the café's Muse-indulgent new hours: *NYITVA 09-24h!* (One of the perhaps blessed things about profit, I realize, is that you can make more of it if you keep longer hours.)

The prices, of course, *have* gone up: An espresso that was once 35 *forints* is now 50, a *briós* that was 25 in December up a whopping 60% to 40 today. It's small potatoes to me, but—I remind myself, thinking of the unshaven, eighty-year-old retired man I saw the other day in the *Café Lukács,* peddling his library books from table to table—for many of my Hungarian friends it may be the difference between going out and staying home. But the décor, at least, is blessedly the same, the plaque on the wall proudly announcing that the furnishings are antiques of museum quality.

And then there's yet another "improvement" that seems to me—a man in his forties trying his best to concentrate on his work—a dubious victory for private enterprise: The former waitresses—a group of mostly friendly, physically unstartling, middle-aged women—have all been replaced by (forgive me, my feminist friends) a group of young knock-outs, so that now—as the gorgeous young waitress, more things bobbing as she walks than merely my cup, brings me my coffee, it's not just the restlessness of incipient creation that courses through my veins, but the slight unease of incinerated desire—something the previous waitresses here allowed me to leave momentarily behind. Could it be, I wonder, that in a "market" economy there's no longer room for the homely, the mid-aged, the pock-marked, the conventionally unglamorous?

BRAVE NEW WORLD

Shut up and drink your coffee, I say to myself, *get to work.* It's only, after all, life once again: Mixed and ambiguous; full of mystery and contradictions; resistant, as ever, to ideology and ideologists; always making you tremble with one thing or another, desire or disgust, or both.

MAY 1993

WHEN FREEDOM'S
JUST ANOTHER WORD
FOR SOMETHING LEFT TO LOSE

My title, as many readers will recognize, is merely a take-off from an old song made popular by Janis Joplin ("Freedom's just another word for *nothing* left to lose"), but my theme, I like to think, is contemporary, having just returned to Budapest after a summer away to find the American market economy's inexorable march toward that elusive word ("freedom") alive and well.

The *Oktogon*, for example (whose eight corners, forever hereafter, will evoke in my mind those eight pinnacles of consumer freedom—*McDonald's, Burger King, Pizza Hut, Dunkin' Donuts, Kentucky Fried Chicken, Reebok, Bon-Bon Hemingway,* and—our very latest addition on the local scene—*Wendy's*), more and more resembles that by-now-clichéed stretch of highway that leads into any town in the American West (whose theory of development, in "pre-ecological" times, could be paraphrased as: *"We've got the space—why worry?"*).

Meanwhile, the French—those overly romantic and retrograde Neanderthals who worry about such trivialities as the quality of sensual life and the preservation of a traditional culture—are more and more the butt of jokes on editorial pages (i. e., *Time*, October 4, 1993) and in corporate board rooms all over the West, as they find it, to quote Thomas Sancton in the aforementioned article, "hard to adjust to a world" wherein culture is universally produced by Hollywood, food by Madison Avenue, and literature by Stephen King and Danielle Steele.

It is interesting, however, to note that—at one and the same time that all this consumer and cultural bounty threatens to engulf (or, as some would prefer to put it, *enrich*) both Western *and* Central/Eastern Europe, it is not merely the French who are proving so perversely ungrateful. It is also the Eastern Europeans, who (perhaps as a way of registering at the ballot box their disapproval of the homogenization of culture and the de-homogenization of wealth that "free" market economies so frequently signify), in increasing numbers and in an increasing number of countries—Poland, Bulgaria, Russia, Romania, even to some extent here in Hungary—seem to be evincing a certain nostalgia for their imperfect, but in many ways more secure, socialist pasts.

This suggests, perhaps, as we have always known, that one man's (or woman's) freedom is another's enslavement, one person's choice another's absence of choice. For "freedom" (*szabadság*), indeed—much like "choice" (*választék*)—is one of *any* language's most ambiguous words to define, as the title of William Styron's famous novel (*Sophie's Choice*) ought aptly to illustrate. As the philosopher John Dewey once put it, "Freedom of action without freed capacity of thought behind it is only chaos."

When Thomas Sancton chastises the French by arguing that "the French public overwhelmingly *chooses* American images—just as it *chooses* blue jeans and Coca-Cola," it is a rather naive understanding of the nuances of both language and the human psyche (rather than a deep understanding of the French, or of culture in general) he displays. If you have been taught your entire life to equate American culture, American food, American values, and American economics, with the "good" life, and your own with the "bad," then the "choice" between a *káposzta saláta* and a Whopper, or, for that matter, a *Túró Rudi* and a Mars bar—no matter how great the disparities in price and/or nutritive value—doesn't seem much like a choice after all.

It is, of course, easy, and inviting—as the mere "tourist" living abroad for a time who will return, presumably, to his happy nest of efficiency and two hundred kinds of toothpaste—to wax philosophical about such matters as cultural integrity, sensual pleasure, social justice and the like.

And these are, of course, also not the best of times for those of us who remain unapologetic socialists…or, at least, unapologetic social democrats. But the equation, in some minds at least, of the presence of Wendy's with the absence of the Secret Police, of the ubiquity of Stephen King with the death of the censor, may, in the end, say as much about their *mis*understanding of language as their understanding of politics.

And, as for *this* writer at least: "Waiter—another *káposzta saláta* and a *somlói galuska,* please."

SEPTEMBER 1993

FOR WHOM THE BELL TOLLS

Imagine yourself in this situation:

You are a university student taking something like eighteen hours of classes weekly in any five or six of no fewer than ninety separate buildings scattered around a city. Not unoccasionally, several classes, each of which is one of your graduation requirements, are held at conflicting time and/or locations, so that you—quite literally—need to miss one to attend the other.

Your professors—almost all of whom make, if they're lucky, somewhere around 30,000 *forints* net—roughly $250 U.S.—a month, and each of whom holds between one and three other jobs (translating, editing, teaching business English, etc.) to support his/her family, are, understandably enough, rarely around—not so much unapproachable as, for their own survival, unavailable.

You yourself—who, if you're lucky, receive a monthly stipend of about a third of your professor's salary—also must work at several part-time jobs (usually teaching English, French or Spanish) if you are to make ends meet, and you find yourself, on a typical day, running between somewhere like, say, Pesti Barnabás utca, Ajtósi Dürer sor, Astoria, Izabella utca, Szerb utca, and—if you still have enough energy, or desire, left for a private life—perhaps your boyfriend's or girlfriend's, or down-town for a beer (if you can afford it—which you probably can't).

What you will do with all this—if you are, say, in the humanities—is still a mystery. Teach and work at two other jobs like your professors? Leave the country? Wait it out for teaching and/or intellectual life to become "respectable" professions in a newly created market economy? Try and find a job waiting on tables at *Café Gerbeaud?*

Is it any wonder, then, that what you're most concerned about is not really learning, not really getting good grades or taking pride in your work, not the nurturing and stimulation of your intellectual and/or spiri-tual life, but—above all—that treasured signature of your professor on the line adjacent to his or her course signifying the *raison d'etre* for your being there: *You got the credit.* In and out, that's what you most want—the piece of paper that will at least "license" you, even margin-ally, to earn a living. Irrelevant, really, whether the grade is a *jeles* (A), a *jó* (B), a *közepes* (C), or a *elégséges* (D). Not because you are cynical or depraved or superficial, but because a system in which there is so little time—because (and here's a good illustration of Market Economics 101 for you) there's so little *money*—for real thought or learning has, willy nilly, made you that way.

"What is it like to teach at a Central European university?" is, quite naturally, one of the most frequent questions I've gotten since arriving here, and the above little narrative will perhaps tell you something of the answer. Having gone from the world's richest university—a univer-sity older, even, than the country it resides in, a university with a staff of full-time "development officers" sufficient to populate a small army—to one of the world's poorest (a university at which most of our infre-quent department meetings are about the raising of money; at which professors must, for the most part, buy their own pens and papers, pay their own postage; at which it was suggested at our first department meeting last fall that faculty be limited to one hundred pages of Xerox paper for the semester!), the answer should, perhaps, be self-evident. For it is a system where—financially, infra-structurally, humanly, politi-cally—almost everything militates against the tranquillity and peace of mind intellectual work requires. A system where—as is typical of any market economy, new or old—you can tell a great deal about a government's, or a society's, priorities by simply tracing the supply of money it invests in its various endeavors.

To argue that there is a simple solution for all this in a society strug-gling on all fronts to re-orient itself to a market economy in a constantly changing world would be an act of extreme naiveté, if not downright romanticism. The choices are never quite as simple as the rhetoric of guns or butter, libraries or Burger Kings, might suggest.

Yet one thing, ultimately, is eminently clear: When teachers' salaries are frozen at the unconscionably low levels at which the present government is seeking to freeze them, the development of minds, hearts, and souls is frozen in the same cold chill. And, last week, when those 2,000-odd teachers demonstrated against the government's pay freeze outside the Academy of Science, another group should have been there demonstrating as well—the students, for whom the same bell's dark and unconscionable ringing tolls as well.

JULY 1993

ELECTION POSTSCRIPT:
THE (UN)WISDOM
OF (IN)SECURITY

The first round of the Hungarian elections is now past, concluding a rather staggering victory for the socialists (with an absolute socialist majority in the second round, even according to my friends in SZDSZ, highly likely). It is now time for the pundits, one of whom I will herein pretend to be, to offer their analyses and explanations of these events, falsely interpreted in much as the Western press as a return to the Communist past, but correctly interpreted by some, I think, as signaling a triumph of the wish for security over the need for unbridled market freedoms and adventures.Indeed, one of the more superficial pieties of free-market systems—namely, that of the direct relationship between spending and outcome—was dramatically turned on its head in the recent campaign, with the MSZP (proving themselves, ironically enough, successful "investors" after all) garnering 32.9% of the votes for only 4.7% of the campaign spending, compared with rampantly free-market FIDESZ's 7.5% and 31% respectively. What these figures suggest is that it was *not* familiarity, or even specificity of program, voters were voting for, but something deeper, more abstract, and—whether or not ultimately wise—worth heeding for Hungarian politicians of the present and future.

Indeed, it might be said that, in this post-1989 "new world" of Eastern and Central Europe, one of the more obvious challenges for the new politics consists of whether, and how, it can combine the obviously costly (and, in some cases, economically and psychologically lethal) securities offered by the previous regimes with the ever-seductive freedoms and opportunities suggested by the industrialized free-market West—the same West, we must remind ourselves, which now finds itself with rampant double-digit unemployment ranging from just under 10% in Belgium to a whopping 20% in once-romantic Spain.

Behind those depressing numbers, as these recent elections should remind us, are not merely ideologies, but people—real flesh-and-blood human beings with mouths to feed, psyches to stabilize, self-esteem and personal tranquillity to hunger for—people who vote not so much for systems as for situations, people who believe, ultimately, that a sense of security by any other name might smell equally sweet. And it is in this context, perhaps, that we ought to examine the so-called nostalgia for socialism that is presently sweeping Central/Eastern Europe—be it, as in the MSZP, socialism with a decided market economy patina or the more unapologetic, old-school kind that can still be heard from the lips of certain pensioners trying to make do in the "new" world on 8,000 *forints* (roughly $80 U.S.) a month. It is, I suspect, far less a nostalgia for any particular system (real human beings—at least those who aren't writing textbooks and treatises—rarely care about systems) than a nostalgia for that most time-tested and universally longed for human environment, a sense of security. The most ideologically convinced Marxists, after all (as many an American academic can testify) tend to be those with tenure; the most fervent free-market boosters those with trust funds and inherited wealth.

Indeed, one of the great, unchallenged pieties of our time is the idea that most people need, crave, or long for, those great icons of contemporary life known as "challenges" and "opportunities"—external (usually career/money oriented) Holy Grails which people, like untethered Jasons, will make a beeline for if only some malevolent system releases them into the sweet jungle of their private passions and greeds. This callous assumption (made, I've found, almost always by the rich, well-born, and terribly lucky) that the vicissitudes of daily life—of working, suffering, loving, and raising children—don't offer at least enough in the way of challenge to keep most people occupied, is one of America's and the West's greatest legacies to contemporary life, suggesting that the post-modern, ever-changing self is the only one worth having, a new or better (read: "higher-paying") job the only one worth holding.

But something in Hungary's collective psyche these days, as well as in its economic indicators, seems to suggest otherwise, to be saying that, no matter how many different kinds of sneakers a society may produce, if it doesn't also produce secure and stable human lives, no amount of ideological chest-thumping or propagandistic self-congratulation will earn for it the loyalty of its citizens…or their peace of mind.

Given these human and psychological realities, *any* successful post-Communist government—by whatever political or ideological name it might choose to call itself—will need to dedicate itself to those (in fact, very ideologically *American*) principles of "public strength and individual security" Alexander Hamilton once spoke of, that sense of "greater security for the average man" Franklin Roosevelt knew was the hallmark of any society brazen enough to call itself democractic. Free Democrat, Young Democrat, Old Socialist, New Socialist: Call themselves what they will, what those rising numbers in the world's "richest" countries—along with the outcome of the elections here—may be trying to tell us is that it will be a politics of compassion, rather than of ideology, that will—or, rather, *must*—rule the future.

"Men," wrote the great French aphorist La Rouchefoucault, "promise with their hopes, and perform with their fears." And it seems that, with great frequency at least, they vote with them as well, serving to remind us that Alan Watts' Zen-psychological classic of the late '60s— *The Wisdom of Insecurity*—was, after all, not quite a political system, but only a book.

MAY 1994

REACH OUT
AND TOUCH EVERYONE

...there is no new country, no new life
on the globe today. It is the same old thing,
in different degrees, everywhere. *Plus ça
change, plus c'est la meme chose.*

D. H. LAWRENCE
STUDIES IN CLASSIC AMERICAN LITERATURE

We've all, by now, had the experience, though we may have missed
its meaning: You're seated at what you suppose to be a quiet, romantic
restaurant in the Buda hills, trying to have an intimate conversation
with your dinner partner. Suddenly, to your amazement, inches away,
probably at the table behind you, you hear a familiar but most unwelcome sound: The ringing of a telephone...not on the restaurant's reser-
vation line, but smack dab between the knife and soup spoon of the
young business type whom someone has "reached out and touched"

right here, amid the candle-lit once-privacy of *Náncsi Néni's*. Or, alternatively: You're walking along near the *Oktogon* on a bright afternoon, where a post-Orwellian young Turk half your age leans confidently against his shiny new BMW, immersed, you think at first glance, in the possible derangement of talking to himself. But, no, on closer inspection, you're wrong again: He's merely singing to his honey, or arranging a mid-afternoon tryst, or finalizing a deal for widgets from Mongolia, on that latest appendage of modern, post-Communist man (and woman): the cellular phone.

Or, alternatively (if you're younger than I am, and single): You're on your first date with a hot young Hungarian yuppie whom you met the night before at your favorite hang-out, the Hully Gully. After a pair of delectable *almás rétes* (apple strudel) and a few glasses of *fehér bor*(white wine) over at your new, post-modern, expatriate's pad, you're just about to reach out and touch her yourself when—*poof!*—from the recesses of her elsewhere sequestered pocketbook comes an eerily familiar sound: the ringing of a phone. "Oops," says she, pushing you gently away, *"bocsánat,"* and, next thing you know, she's cooing sweetly on her cellular phone to István, and—*wham, bam!*—she's out the door.

Yes, friends, all over Budapest—indeed, all over the now technologically and ideologically re-united world—*the bells are ringing for you and your gal*...and for anyone else who's got your number. Antiquated phone lines? Underdeveloped infrastructure? Weep no more, fair citizens of this ever newer and newer cosmos. And for those of us who simply, now and then, like a little peace and quiet, a few moments' reprieve from Internet and Infrastructure, Musak and Modem, there is now the Central/Eastern European equivalent to the American non-smoker's nemesis of passive smoke: the passive telephone call. What was once, at worst, an unwelcome intrusion into the privacy of your own home is now, at best, an aggravating nuisance in the ever-expanding non-privacy of the interconnected world.

Is there nowhere, I wonder as I watch them—on the phone in their cars, on the phone on the streets, on the phone on the train, on the phone in the air, on *two* phones at once (one on each ear), on the phone beneath the quaking Aspen—that is still safe for us technological Neanderthals, we refugees from Internet and Intercom, Intel and Comtel, E-mail, phone-mail, IBM and PCBs?

"Every day," the American farmer/ecologist/writer Wendell Berry (a *true* cro-magnon, who still farms with horses and uses a manual typewriter) once wrote, "do something that won't compute." But what, I wonder, as the entire cosmos (to make a bad paraphrase of once-LSD-guru Timothy Leary's ancient advice) drops in, tunes in, and turns on their machines and everyone else's, is there *left* to do that won't compute? Where is there left to *go* where someone can't, if you don't want them to, "reach out and touch" you...or where you might, with Melville's Bartleby, "prefer not to" listen to the intimate wheelings and dealings of the young entrepreneur at the table beside you?

"Once upon a time there was a path, then a road, then a highway, then an information highway," might go the Pollyanna-ish history of our times as written by that great American ecologist, Al Gore. It's, after all (just ask anyone), the new mega-bitten face of the new universal democracy: Information for everyone and anyone, all they can eat, anywhere and everywhere. And, like every democracy, it has its have-nots and want-nots, its grouchy bad citizens who would rather hear a warbler than a dial tone, rather go get their mail from the mailbox than a computer, rather go to the library and interact with a real human being than turn on a switch and manipulate (oh God!) a "mouse."

"The majority of men lead lives of quiet desperation," wrote yet another Neanderthal, Henry David Thoreau, whom this very week I have been teaching and recommending to my Hungarian students on the theory that his appeal to the young (and to their un-resigned elders) lies in the fact that he, along with his friend Emerson, dared to ask the fundamental question: *How shall I live?* But what happens when their desperation gets so noisy, the instruments of it so ubiquitous, the static from them so droning and relentless (I haven't yet gotten around to mentioning that other new ear-shattering invention, the automobile anti-theft device) that they threaten to drown out, to pollute the very air of, the rest of us?

Oh, silly, aging, post-romantic boy, wasting all this energy and *animus* on what is already a *fait accompli?* Why not just relax, enjoy the new Central/Eastern Europe, turn on your computer and read your mail? It's a new life, after all, isn't it? Or, at the very least, the same old world, still begging to be new.

NOVEMBER 1994

Postscript: Some three days after placing the last period on the above essay, I was teaching my American Literature Seminar at ELTE when, suddenly, from the depths of one of my female students' pocketbook, that eerily familiar sound injected itself into our discussion of Hawthorne's *Scarlet Letter*. With only a slight blush of embarrassment, the student reached into her bag, took out the shiny plastic source of our *educatus interruptus,* excused herself, and went out into the hall. *To hell with the Puritans,* I thought I heard her whisper under her breath as she left.

ELEGY FOR THE LÁNGOS

Let's face it, if a young man invites a woman
out, will she want to eat a *lángos* at a stand
or hamburger in a shiny new restaurant?

HUNGARIAN JOURNALIST ERNŐ BAJOR NAGY,
BEMOANING THE KILLING OFF OF TRADITIONAL
HUNGARIAN *LÁNGOS* BY AMERICAN FAST FOOD

It is a soft and chewy food, perfect for a hunger that knows no limits,
so resplendent with oil that, like a lover's sweat in late August, it literally oozes out at you when you take a bite. If, on a brisk morning in
mid-January (or, for that matter, on any other morning), you take the
#56 tram or bus to its final stop along Huvösvölgyi út and take a few
steps up the hill to your right, you can find one of Budapest's best,
topped (for those who are cholesterol-impervious, or merely risk-tak-
ers) with *tejföl* and *sajt* (sour cream and cheese), and so warm and
chewy you can fold it like a wool glove in the palm of your hand, sa-
voring one of the last remaining icons of Hungary's pre-capitalist past,
yet another dying relic that—like the brothels and small shopkeepers
being replaced by Burger Kings and Pizza Huts—will soon be the subject only of nostalgic films and romantic memoirs, a symbol of the lardy,

socialist past that is slowing going the way of all flesh…the way of Newt Gingrich, the way of Bob Dole.

But the *lángos* (pronounced **lang**-*osh*), of course (for a writer, at least) is a metaphor as well, as were the small electrical and pharmaceutical shops across the street from my studio recently replaced by a New York Bagels, as was the "old" Anna Café on Váci utca recently replaced by the pricey, upscale "new" Anna Café ("an old world feeling," reads the advertisement, "that feels right today"—at five times the price!), as was the *Eötvös Klub* on Irányi utca, recently converted to an unspeakably glitzy and noisy Wizard's *Játék* Center, selling—you guessed it—New York Bagels.

One's man's (or woman's) decline, the rule of life seems to have it, is another's progress, the latter term once defined by the writer and historian Samuel Butler as "based upon a universal innate desire on the part of every organism to live beyond its income." So that the apparent demise of the *lángos* and triumph of the hamburger (and of the bagel, the Dunkin' Donut, and the greasy pizza) are merely, one could argue, examples of the world's immutable cycle of death and resurrection being enacted on our very streets. Yet life, as Samuel Johnson pointed out, is "a progress from want to want, *not* from enjoyment to enjoyment," so it might be worthwhile contemplating what it is we are replacing with what and whether Ernő Bajor Nagy's only half-fictitious girl will really be happier, once she gets there, at her shiny new restaurant than at the *lángos* stand on Huvösvölgy út.

I myself (a New York Jewish boy, after all) have nothing at all against bagels (or against the two enterprising young guys, both graduates of the university I taught at, who brought them here) finding myself—against, I must confess, some of my own better instincts—irresistibly drawn to my corner bagel bakery when my craving for a *lángos* (no longer available in my rapidly yuppifying neighborhood) is, all too easily, replaced by my nostalgia for cream cheese. Yet, when I enter the New York Bagels on Bajcsy-Zsilinszky út—as when I enter any McDonald's or Burger King or Pizza Hut—an uneasy sense of instant anywhere comes over me, a sense that we are, on a world-wide scale, now living out Gertrude Stein's famous description of the city of Oakland: "There is no *there* there."

For, no doubt in an age soon to come—as the *lángos* gives way to the hamburger, the *rétes* to the bagel, Koncz Zsuzsa and Bródy János to Madonna and Michael Jackson, *paprikás csirke* to Kentucky Fried Chicken—the world, grown safe for democracy, will inevitably become

one vast America…"with liberty and justice for all," but without tex-
*ture, diversity, culture, and difference—without, perhaps, a place for our
enthusiastic girl in the shiny new restaurant to feel she is entirely at home.*

Right this very minute she is probably sitting there, her new boyfriend (a replacement for the old one who used to take her to the *lángos*
stand) chatting away on his cellular phone while she inhales a Whopper, an order of fries, and a large Coke, feeling she has finally made it in
the New World. But what, I wonder, will she be thinking ten years from
now, the *lángos* having gone the way of the dinosaur, the small shop-
keeper and retiree having sold off their libraries in the renovated Anna,
everything all cleaned up and perfect and perfectly similar in a world
which—since it no longer knows difference—may no longer know love.

MARCH 1995

HELLO TO ALL THAT

But this happiness remains merely a possible one: for, in our capitalist society, the things promised are not the things owed.

GEORGES PEREC

You have to start around twenty.

FIDEL CASTRO
ON BEING TOO OLD TO BECOME A CAPITALIST

Ships at a distance have every man's wish on board.

ZORA NEALE HURSTON

It seems to be a weakness of our race that, in times of fundamental change, we naively expect to procure the benefits and excitement of the new while magically retaining the securities of the old, a psychological infirmity not without its applications to the (believe it or not, *socialist*) Horn government's recently proposed economic measures here in Hungary.

For it seems rather shocking that, to anyone acquainted with the day-to-day social and economic realities of the Western democracies (the United States in particular), many of these proposals should have come as much of a surprise. Indeed, the same parties who at this very moment are waxing so eloquently against such proposals as the newly proposed university tuition, decreases in social welfare benefits, property taxes, reduced institutional and foundation subsidies, means testing for family allowances, drastically trimmed down maternity benefits and the like—had they bothered to really *examine* those capitalist economies they are now emulating, might have found the same priorities at the very heart of those systems, no less inherent to the matrix of the Western industrialized economies than Burger Kings and Pizza Huts. For it was not merely an abstract dictum of Winston Churchill's that "the inherent vice of capitalism is the unequal sharing of blessings; the inherent virtue of socialism is the equal sharing of miseries"

For better or worse, however, such abstractions ("capitalism" and "socialism") are most often invoked by those who have little day-to-day stake in their stark factual realities—those, for example, in a very different position from my friend Sándor, a taxi driver in Budapest's 14th District who came home from a full-day's work the other day with a bad back and a mere 300 *forints* (less than $3.00 U.S.), and whose wife Eva spends the day at home gluing on pharmaceutical labels for even less; those in a very different position from the woman I met in the optical store the other day who, as I tried on a pair of Austrian-made, 23,000-*forint* ($200.00 U.S.) frames, explained to me that the price of the frames alone was well in excess of her monthly pension; those in a very different position from the elderly woman carrying two tattered shopping bags into the Goethe Institute this very morning, going from table to table trying to sell a few bunches of scraggly narcissus for twenty *forints* (about fifteen cents) each.

To be sure, it hardly appears that these were the only options available to the Horn government for beginning to solve its (largely inherited) economic miseries. A substantial cracking down on the untaxed and underground "black" economy, or an increased tax burden for the wealthy, for example, might have been equally helpful in reducing some of Hungary's huge internal and external debt without unduly penalizing those (workers, retirees, students, etc.) least able to afford it. Yet it also seems that capitalism, as the economist Joseph Schumpeter once observed, "inevitably and by virtue of the very logic of its civilization creates, educates and subsidizes a vested interest in social unrest." And it is that system—and, with it, that logic and that unrest—that presently, by popular demand, straddles the Hungarian nation and the other "newly liberated" countries of this region.

In economics and politics, as in personal life, there is (to borrow the title of a friend's book) "No Heaven," and ideology—while offering a certain verbal and moral aphrodisiac for columnists, politicians, academics and dictators of all sorts—has hardly, if ever, proved a balm to an ordinary citizen, East or West, Communist or post-. Some academics, such as sociologist Daniel Bell in *The End of Ideology,* have, to their credit, always known this. "Capitalism," he wrote in his justly well-known book, "it is said, is a system wherein man exploits man. And communism—is vice versa."

And so now, as Hungarians begin unabstractedly to reap what they may, out of a certain abstract zeal, have sown, it may not be too early to declare as premature economist Robert L. Heilbroner's declaration of victory in an article entitled "The Triumph of Capitalism" (*The New Yorker,* Jan 23, 1989)—to wit, that "less than seventy-five years after it officially began, the contest between capitalism and socialism is over: Capitalism has won." For though it may yet be proven, as Churchill said of democracy, that capitalism is the worst of all systems…until one compares it with every other system—the final truth or untruth of that assumption, I suspect, remains to be seen. But for the moment, and for better or worse, the means for making such very personal and unideological comparisons, here in Hungary and elsewhere throughout Central/Eastern Europe, are slowly falling into place.

MARCH 1995

FAMOUS FOR SIXTEEN SECONDS

Between the poem and the film that costs
a million dollars, it is the poem that endures,
that continues to be written no matter what
the circumstances.

SALMAN RUSHDIE

Alan Parker had seen my video, the Hungarian-accented voice on
the other end of the phone said several weeks ago, and wanted me to
play the part of one of the singing members of Peron's cabinet in "Evita."
So why not? I *had,* in fact—out of the mixed motives that usually char-
acterize our behavior —gone to the auditions here in Budapest several
weeks earlier.

For one, I was curious: What *is* it, in fact, that these Hollywood figures—so ludicrously well paid, so relentlessly showered with media
and other kinds of attention, their every love affair, haircut, and bowel
movement the subject of such intense public scrutiny, who are flown in,

flown out, feted and housed like our own version of royalty—what is it that they actually *do* all day to deserve such wealth and public devotion?

Secondly, like most writers, who spend their professional lives, as I am now, seated alone behind a desk in a well-lit room engaged in the physically rather unglamorous activity of typing, I was looking for an excuse to get out into "the world," that place where those more adept, or perhaps more talented, than myself at social intercourse make their way through the slings and arrows of outrageous fortune.

Thirdly—also, I suspect, like most writers—I'm quite vain, though often too timid or unsure of myself to make a public spectacle of it . If I could hold onto my own personality, my own way of muddling through a day, and *still* be a movie star—well, who wouldn't? So, well, let it suffice to say that, when I saw the advertisement looking for individuals "between the ages of 30 and 70 with interesting-looking faces who could sing and/or dance" to audition for bit parts in "Evita," I had immediately jumped on the absence of the words "handsome" or "beautiful" (having still enough vanity to number myself among these more euphemistically described as "interesting") and on my now-long-ago unsuccessful avocation as a singer in a rock band, to wend my way, on a sunny Saturday morning, into a rather remote corner of Budapest and sing my own personalized cover of "500 Miles" in front of a video camera and downsized British casting crew.

So there I was—my slicked-down hair clipped to the length of a cucumber's, a heavily starched collar forcing my chin towards the ceiling, my rather too-tight black frock coat and vest reminding me that I had been existing on a Hungarian diet for too long—gathered with a group of roughly fifteen other middle-aged and older, mostly Hungarian, men, practicing, in various off-key renditions of cracked English, our sixteen seconds of "the evidence suggests/she has other interests/ if it's her who's using him/he's exceptionally dim."

In the staging area off to a side of Budapest's Ethnographic Museum for what was to be our brief flirtation with Hollywood and fame, we practiced and practiced, smoked, munched on the extra's daily rations of a sausage sandwich, apple, Hungarian muffin and juice, and—mostly—waited. And waited and waited and waited.

Finally, of course, as it is wont to, even in Hollywood, our moment came. Summoned by one of what seemed like hundreds of sub-sub-directors talking to one another through hundreds of walkie talkies, we were marched into the Ethnographic Museum itself, seated around a table at the head of which stood a certain English actor named

Nelson-something, who had been cast in the role of one General Farrell and whose monumental verbal moment in the sun for the entire day of filming consisted of the tri-syllabic sound, *"Release him."* For the umpteenth time, our noses were powdered by Moira the Irish nose-powderer, our cowlicks slicked down by Rose, our shoulders and lapels brushed by Joan the wardrobe master, our buttons and collars checked by a small armada of other wardrobe types, as—with Director Parker and a nearly Bosnian-army-sized task force of sub-, sub-sub-, and other directors, camera people, lighting experts and prop arrangers barking orders and blowing artificial smoke into the air—we proceeded to do no fewer than a dozen takes of General Farrell's soon-to-be-immortalized, *"Release him."*

Now if you, dear reader, detect a trace of envy and cynicism in the above rendition of one aspiring actor's sixteen seconds beneath the lights (the result of what was, in fact, a thirteen-hour work-and-waiting day, paid—for those talented enough to sing—at a whopping $75 U.S.) you are, no doubt, right. For no writer of relatively unread, unavailable, unadvertised and undistributed books such as myself who's in his or her right mind can look lightly, or without a certain degree of envy, on the fame, money, power—above all, the *audience*—that these various moguls and their minions seem able to summon from our superficial culture-starved public.

And now—seated once again in my naturally lit and smokeless room where I am producer and director, cameraman and wardrobe manager, best boy and key grip, all at once, my nose unpowdered, my hair once again the texture of chicory, trying to do my quiet best at this "craft and sullen art" of mine—I have seen, if only for a day, how those so much more beloved, and honored, by our culture spend their time. Surely, life being more of a jungle than a meritocracy, they don't deserve all they get—though who in his or her right mind ever thought otherwise? But of one thing, at least, my sixteen powdered and smokey seconds beneath the lights have convinced me:

They can have it.

January 1996

PART VII

AMERICA THROUGH NEW EYES

ELECTION POSTSCRIPT: PROUD TO BE AN AMERICAN AGAIN

For those of us who came of political and intellectual age in the '60s, inspired as we were by that era's vision of social and economic justice and community, the twelve years of the Reagan-Bush era have been a dirty dozen indeed, tempting many of us who were once instructed by our more conservative fellow citizens (*vis a vis* America) to "love it or leave it" to contemplate the latter, the former having grown increasingly difficult.

Indeed, among the many other incentives for spending a period of time in another culture, not least of those which fueled my own pilgrimage to Hungary was the wish to be, at least temporarily, in a culture in which capitalism and free enterprise might once again be associated with hope and opportunity rather than with the increasingly distressing and morally repugnant gap between rich and poor, rhetoric and fact, that has marked the last twelve years of American social and economic reality.

Indeed, I remember all too well the sense of hope and pride I felt when, after working on Jimmy Carter's Inauguration in 1976, I watched our newly sworn-in President and his wife dismount from the Presidential limousine and, holding hands, walk down Pennsylvania Avenue, a gesture rightfully intended as a metaphor for the kinder, less imperial (though at the time unappreciated) administration that was to come.

President Carter, in the meantime, fell from grace and, like the good Christian he is, was resurrected—the latter not so much thanks to the media or other historical revisionists as to his own morally exemplary behavior since leaving the Oval Office, in striking contrast to the typically Republican golf-and-martini retirements of his predecessor and successor. And history, eternally more reliable than the temporary vicissitudes of public opinion, has already begun (given the ravages of social and economic justice that were to follow) to look considerably more kindly upon Carter's presidency, just as it is already beginning to reconsider the mean-spirited economic "wonders" of the Reagan-Bush years.

For myself at least, America—the land that saved the lives of my parents (from Nazi Germany); the land that had once reached out to the world, asking it to give her "your tired, your poor, your huddled masses yearning to be free"—became, during the last twelve years, an almost morally unbearable place to inhabit, a mere relic of the once-bountiful shelter that now seemed predominantly home to the greedy, the homeless (whom it helped to create), the poorly educated, the cynical, and the temporarily disillusioned. Under the transparently hollow rhetoric of "kinder and gentler," my country had become, instead, colder and harsher, crueler and more unfeeling; my students more interested in *net*working than working; my neighbors more concerned with expanding their portfolios than their spirits. Nor did one need to go very far to accumulate the evidence: The dramatically increasing gap between rich and poor (with the most affluent 1% of the population now accounting for 60% of the nation's wealth); the dramatic increase in infant mortality and poverty among the young (with as many as a quarter of American children under the age of eighteen living in poverty); the increasing abandonment of any real concern (and support) for public education; the utterly deplorable record, compared with the rest of the developed world, as to maternity leave and child benefits for working parents. And one didn't need to rely solely on figures: The evidence of the decline in our national "character" (a word President Bush misused so reprehensibly to attack Clinton during the campaign) was right there at our doorsteps, on our streets, huddled over sewer covers and heating grates, reaching out to us from the mock-warmth of our subway tunnels.

But now, at last, that time—a time which, I am certain, will come to be known (to paraphrase President Roosevelt's description of the Japanese attack of Pearl Harbor) as a time of "infamy" in our national history—is finally over: A Democrat—one who, in the great tradition of modern Democrats (not perfect by any means, but at least *human*), seems willing to pay more than lip service to questions of social and economic justice and equal opportunity—is once again in The White House.

And America—the country I love, much as I did as a young, idealistic student in the 1960s (when, unlike Bill Clinton, I *did* inhale), the country I was glad to leave just a few months ago has now made me look forward, proudly, to going back. For the torch has been handed once again, not to a *new* generation of Americans, but to the same, slighter older one that made me proud to be an American to begin with.

JANUARY 1993

TALE OF TWO SCHOOLS

Every step toward some wished-for Eden, not only life but history inevitably teaches us, is a step away from yet another paradise, perhaps more real. And the conviction, *a priori,* that "ours" is better—whether it's schools, cars, hamburgers, or political systems we speak of—is only the flip side of the hubristic assumption that *we,* somehow, are better as well. Yet it's not been infrequently over the past two years that various American friends and colleagues have stared at my wife and me with a bewilderment bordering on pity when we've informed them that (despite the fact that the Fulbright Commission was obligated to pay for his tuition at a private American school) our three-year-old son attended a Hungarian *óvoda*…as though, perhaps, we were voluntarily subjecting him to a kind of cultural torment, a sensory deprivation he would never recover from.

"Why would you do *that?*" they ask. "The American schools here are so much better?" Or: "Aren't you worried about his not speaking English?" Or: "Aren't you afraid he'll wind up 'behind' the other kids when you get back to the States?" Nonetheless, in my thus-far nearly two years in Hungary, one of the repeated, and repeating, episodes of unambivalent "rightness" I have experienced, it seems to me, has been the hour of retrieving my son from the warm, capable hands of Vali, Vilma and Juli along Városligeti fasor, where—amidst an admitted modesty of material goods and choices—I sense he is receiving the one thing no mere "market" economy can provide, the one endowment no amount of dollars can purchase: a calm and supportive atmosphere of tolerance, humor, and love.

So my wife and I recently found ourselves, once again, feeling somewhat "foreign" and on the defensive when we attended the annual Christmas Fair and Book Sale at the American School of Budapest, a place filled with the kind of plenitude and good cheer that has come, in the eyes of much of the non-Western world, to symbolize America. Yet, once there, a gray cloud of fatigue and depression—accompanied, I must confess, by a slightly self-satisfied sense of victory—came over us. For we sensed, somehow—behind this other so well-endowed institution, behind the preponderance of books, toys, objects, and gadgets compared with our son's modest and relatively barren *óvoda*—a kind of emptiness…the same kind of emptiness which, in part, we had fled America to escape.

This is not to say (for how could I claim to know, based on my single brief visit?) that a loving and supportive atmosphere (along with its more obvious bounty of goods and alternatives) is not provided by the American school(s) here as well. Or that both material *and* emotional largesse can't co-exist in a single place. (I'm neither so incurable a romantic, nor so confirmed a socialist.) Yet I feel a certain relief and—why deny it?—a certain pride at the choice we made, both for ourselves and for our son.

For here—in his humble yet perfectly adequate *Magyar óvoda*, in a world of slightly less Lego and Duplo, of slightly more fat and slightly less protein—though he may already be slightly less ready for Exeter and Harvard than his peers in the hills of Buda, my son may be growing slightly more ready for life.

For he is learning (aside from the reading, writing, arithmetic and new age communications skills which will, inevitably, come) that trust, affection and human generosity have neither borders nor specific language nor allegiance to any single economic or political system…nor can they necessarily be purchased at a higher price. He is learning—in an atmosphere some might call impoverished, but I would call more than adequately bountiful—that, in the words of the American poet Richard Wilbur, it is "love"—not things—that "calls us to the things of this world"; that toys, pardon the joke, 'r *not* us.

Best of all (at least from a poet and writer's point of view), he is experiencing, daily, the beautiful music of a language not entirely his own. And his parents—by coming into contact with Hungarians they might otherwise never have known, with a place they might otherwise never have experienced out of some insular attempt to stick to their 'own' kind—are learning something as well.

So, as we wend our way back down from the cleaner, more well-endowed hills of Buda to the dustier, more modest flatlands of Pest, I feel grateful, not merely for what we have, but for what we don't. Grateful that, here in Hungary, my son has learned more than just *kicsit magyarul* (a little Hungarian): He has also learned something about love.

DECEMBER 1993

Teachers at Noah Blumenthal's pre-shool *(óvoda)* in
Budapest's 7th District, Városligeti fasor #29, June 1996.

PRIMER FOR HUNGARIAN JOURNALISTS: WHAT *NOT* TO LEARN FROM AMERICA

It's often been said (at least by me) that if you want to discover what's most insipid about any culture, all you need to do is turn on your television set. Suffering from such severe back pain recently that I found myself entirely devoid of other spiritual and/or intellectual resources, I therefore decided to turn on NBC's highly-rated TODAY show, hoping to find out something of what was going on "back home."

Alas, I found out. For a full twenty minutes (though it seemed an eternity), I was subjected, first, to a furrow-browed discussion of the latest rumors concerning President Clinton's marital infidelities, and then—as if to suggest that the viewers' appetites for the trivial may not yet have been fully exhausted—to a live four-minute video from California of none other than America's second most important public personage, the drug-ravaged and surgically reconstituted Michael Jackson, emphatically denying (to the extent, that is, that one so obviously sleep-deprived and chemically enhanced is capable of being emphatic) allegations of his own recent pederastic philanderings in the many bed-rooms of his California ranch.

That what Mencken called "the virulence of the [American] national appetite for bogus revelation" is utterly insatiable, or that much of what is licensed in the name of *any* freedom (be it sexual, literary, political, or journalistic) is precisely that which most tends to undermine it, are hardly new insights. But to watch American television for any length of time is, as American media critic Neil Postman points out, to be re-minded of George Bernard Shaw's remark on first seeing the glittering lights of Times Square at night: It must be beautiful, Shaw said, as long as you can't read.

Perhaps it was my own physical pain and exhaustion that rendered these twenty minutes of the American television media particularly in-sipid, that also reminded me of Jean Cocteau's remark that stupidity is always amazing to behold, no matter how often one has encountered it. For even from within a consciousness ravaged by low-priced Hun-garian pharmaceuticals, it seemed to me almost incredible that—at a time when such urgent national and international issues as health care and welfare reform, gun control and a surging crime rate, education reform, a brutal and ongoing genocide in Bosnia, and the possible inte-gration of Central/Eastern Europe into the NATO alliance are at stake—our television media can possibly occupy itself with the conjugal habits of the President or the sexual meanderings of a developmentally ar-rested child billionaire.

By way of a perhaps crude analogy, the junk—almost exclusively—Americans are fed by their so-called television journalists—justified as it is (as are McDonald's, Burger King, etc.) by the fact that the public seems willing, indeed eager, to devour it—is a bit like feeding trash to starving Somalian children: *They're hungry,* our benefactors in the me-dia argue self-righteously. *They'll eat it.* Yet America, these days—and, with it, American print journalism and television—is all the rage...in Eastern and Western Europe, in the former Soviet Union, in most of what was once condescendingly referred to as the Third World and which now aspires to become, like Burger King itself, a single world, homogenized and indivisible, connected not by acts of charity and com-passion, but by e-mail and telecommunications "highways."

But before the Hungarian media (with or without a new media law, with or without a new government) goes all overboard in imitation of its brethren among the American fourth estate, they might do well to remind themselves that responsible journalism, at its best, ought to aspire to that greater art which it, once more according to Mencken, is in such a hurry to imitate—namely, literature. It ought, therefore, *not* to pander to the worst within our admittedly restricted consciousness, but to foster what is most noble, most elevated, within it. And, in doing so, it might remind itself of the most fundamental duty of the free press in a democracy anywhere: To act as the guardian, *not* of whom the president sleeps with, but of how well its citizens sleep.

FEBRUARY 1994

JE CHANGE, DONC JE SUIS: SOME REFLECTIONS ON PROTEANISM AS AN AMERICAN VALUE

A TALK DELIVERED AT A CONFERENCE ON
AMERICAN VALUES AT EÖTVÖS LORÁND UNIVERSITY

America has been called not only "the country of the second chance" but also the country of the "twice-born," a phrase brought into the common vernacular by the American philosopher William James in order to describe those who have found, in the spiritual realm, a second life. As someone who himself has taken advantage of more than his share of second chances, both personally and professionally, I would like to try to describe, from the vantage point of a writer and literary person, some of the qualities that have made America the fluid, indeed—to borrow a phrase from Robert Jay Lifton's recent book, *The Protean Self*— the *protean* nation that it is, and, traditionally, has been.

When History Enters the House

In recent times, you may have observed, the phrase "twice born" has taken on a more secular, even a political, flavor—a flavor in which a second-rate B-movie Hollywood actor can be born again as governor of California, and then as President, or in which, as during the '60s, a once-tenured Harvard experimental psychologist named Timothy Leary could be born again as the psychedelic guru of an entire generation, or in which former Watergate burglars like G. Gordon Liddy can be born again as television evangelists, or a former member of the radical left-wing Chicago Seven can be born again as a three-piece-suited investment banker, or, even more recently, the former Communications Director of the Reagan and Bush White Houses, David Gergen, can be born again, magically, as the Great Explainer of the Clinton Presidency. Just recently, in fact, we bade adieu for the final time to one of the great protean personalities of our time, Richard Nixon, who was declared dead and buried as a national disgrace in August of 1974, only to be revived and reburied as a respected elder statesman in April of 1994. *"Je change,"* these people all seem to be saying to us, *"donc je suis."*

America is, indeed, a generous and forgiving country, a country in which the term "past lives" hardly needs to be taken as a reference to reincarnation, a nation in which virtually every citizen can sing along with Walt Whitman, "I am large, I contain multitudes." Americans, in fact, have been defined by one of their own citizens, the journalist and writer Lewis Lapham, as people who are "always on the way to someplace else," a definition which, we might note, collides metaphysically with Ralph Waldo Emerson's ominous warning that "my giant goes with me wherever I go."

Nonetheless, "America, The Protean Nation" is, rightfully, the title of one of the chapters of Robert Jay Lifton's recent book, a description which takes its title from the Greek sea-god Proteus who was able to change form to fit the exigencies of any occasion. "Were Proteus to change his dwelling place from the seas that fed the Greek imagination," Lifton writes, "he would undoubtedly retire to those that embrace America." And who, I wonder, could blame him? For, as a nation with hardly (at least, compared with the Eastern/Central Europe of our present venue) a history to speak of, even in terms of non-geologic time, a nation which has made the U-Haul van into its vehicle of choice, the airport and the mobile home its most stable sources of permanent domicile, America itself is the incarnation of flux and change, a whole nation seeming to cry out with the poet Keats, "I have no self. I am all selves and none."

It is in these very terms that the American historian and former Librarian of Congress Daniel Boorstin defines the American past, maintaining that "no prudent man dared to be too certain of exactly who he was or what he was about; everybody had to be prepared to become someone else. To be ready for such perilous transmigrations," Boorstin concludes, "was to become an American."

"I resist anything better than my own diversity," Walt Whitman, that most American of poets, wrote in *Leaves of Grass*, and it is as if, ever since, the whole nation has been singing those words with him. Medical school at 45, the Peace Corps at 70, marriage at 90, bungie jumping at 100—in America it all seems not merely possible, but advisable, as if mortality itself could be forced to take a back seat to the ever-resilient American proclivity for change. "I am an American," says the protagonist of Saul Bellow's classic contemporary novel, *The Adventures of Augie March*, echoing Whitman as the novel opens, "Chicago born... and go at things as I have taught myself, free-style, and will make a record in my own way." Later in the novel he exclaims, "I touched all sides, and nobody knew where I belonged." This protean quality of American life, and of the American spirit, may also explain not only Thoreau's much-touted and commented-upon sedentary and contemplative life at Walden Pond but also his restlessness in leaving: "I left the woods for as good a reason as I went there," he writes in *Walden*. "Perhaps it seemed to me that I had several more lives to live, and could not spare any more time for that one."

For Proteus, the god of change and transformation, stands for what Emerson referred to as "keeping the soul liquid," or, in the words of the novelist Ralph Ellison, both for America's "rich diversity and its almost magical fluidity and freedom," and for the "illusion which must be challenged, as Menelaus did in seizing Proteus." And it is precisely this challenge which forces America, again in Ellison's words, to "surrender its insight, its truth [which] lies in its diversity and swiftness of change."

This quality of proteanism, ironically enough, is—despite America's widespread reputation, and indeed history, as a Protestant nation, a fundamental, age-old quality of Jewish mysticism, as interpreted by the great contemporary Jewish scholar Adin Steinsaltz. "If anything is clear," he writes about man's evolution in his famous discourse, *The Thirteen Petalled Rose*, "it is that a rigid, unchanging way is wrong. This principle of movement, of constant change, is the principle manifested by the soul itself in its life on earth."

When History Enters the House

Now, speaking as someone whose own resumé includes such diverse and seemingly contradictory occupations as lawyer, psychotherapist, speechwriter, television producer, arts administrator, poet, novelist, university professor and German teacher, I can't help but confess to my own prejudice in favor of the American capacity to embrace and encourage change, to honor what I think of as the almost undeniable fact that the human being is a complex and evolving organism, no more at home in the fierce specialization into which much of the world forces it than is a planet in a single fixed point in its orbit. We ARE, in fact, large, and DO, in fact, contain, if not multitudes, at least the potential for many different lives; and one of the contemporary geniuses of America, I would argue, has been in its living enactment of these human possibilities, its encouraging of the self to resist fixity and stasis in favor of evolution and development. As Tocqueville wrote of Americaover a century ago,

> Political principles, laws, and human institutions seem malleable, capable of being shaped and combined at will…. A course almost without limits, a field without horizon, is revealed: the human spirit rushes forward and traverses them in every direction…. Fortunes, opinions and laws are there in ceaseless variation: it is as if immutable Nature herself were mutable, such are the changes worked upon her by the hand of man.

But Tocqueville also knew, as did his slightly younger American contemporary Emerson, that in life as in literature, "nothing is free," that the freedom to constantly reinvent the self can be dangerous as well as electrifying. "Thus," he wrote, "not only does democracy make every man forget his ancestors, but it hides his descendants and separates his contemporaries from him; it throws him back forever upon himself alone, and threatens in the end to confine him entirely within the solitude of his own heart." Ultimately, he continues elsewhere, "the spectacle of this excited community becomes monotonous, and, after having watched the moving pageant for a time, the spectator is tired of it …. The aspect of American society is animated, because men and things are always changing; but it is monotonous, because"—

and here he seems to be echoing Tolstoy's conviction about happy families—"all these changes are alike."

Yet there may also, I suspect, be a certain grain of jealousy hidden within this rather intelligent philosophizing—the jealousy of a citizen of a rather rigid, 19th-century society surveying a just-born and highly fluid one, the jealousy, perhaps, of a middle-aged man watching young lovers kiss on Budapest's Margaret Island. For it may be a radical oversimplification, both on Tolstoy's and on Tocqueville's part, to view all happy families *or* all those capable of radical change as, somehow, "alike," merely a foil for the speaker's own inability to achieve either one.

For America's proteanism, as Lifton points out, and especially the con-man quality frequently associated with it, "is inseparable from the nation's status as a land of promise," inseparable from the Jeffersonian American idea, no doubt inherited from the Greeks, that intelligence and capacity, much like a mobile home itself, are transferable from venue to venue, occupation to occupation, identity to identity.

"You are of the opinion, Judge Temple," wrote that more-American-than-America-itself American writer, James Fenimore Cooper, "that a man is to be qualified by nature and education to do only one thing well, whereas I know that genius will supply the place of learning, and that a certain sort of man can do anything and everything."

Just after I typed the above words, in fact, I came upon an article in the local *Budapest Sun* describing exactly the kind of protean individual Cooper and Lifton are speaking of, the dean of the International Management Center in Budapest, Robert Crane. *"Novel dean is not all business,"* read the headline describing Crane's career achievements and changes, among which are having once been recognized as the foremost expert on 19th-century prostitutes in French literature; teaching English in France; being trained by Malaysian aborigines in the art of shooting poison darts; publishing several books on international business practices; and developing a proposal to erect tents for the poor in India, an experience which allowed him to secure a letter of recommendation from Mother Theresa.

Another such protean personality, a close friend of my own, is Harvard psychiatrist John Mack, who may, perhaps, become well known through his recently published book *Abduction: Encounters with Aliens*. A classically trained Freudian psychoanalyst, Mack first broke with the classical orthodoxies of his own profession some twenty-five years ago by writing a Pulitzer Prize-winning biography of yet another protean personality, T. E. Lawrence, better known as Lawrence of Arabia, entitled

Prince of Darkness, then, in the 1970s and '80s, became even more estranged from the psychiatric Tocquevilles and Tolstoys by getting involved in research into psychedelic experiences and altered states of consciousness, as well as in the anti-nuclear and international peace movements as founder of Cambridge Hospital's Center for Psychological Studies in the Nuclear Age. More recently, some three years ago, he became interested—against the cautionary advice of many friends and colleagues who advised him that, *this* time at least, he was going "too far"—in the experiences of those who claimed to have been abducted by aliens in UFOs, proceeding to work with nearly one hundred such individuals, both through hypnosis and otherwise, in his private psychiatric practice, and leading him to write his just-published, carefully researched book about the abduction experience.

That this Protean changeability of Americans and American life can seem, at best, mystifying, if not downright surreal, particularly to a citizen of what was not long ago the "old" Eastern/Central Europe is clearly demonstrated in the following quotation from a wonderful memoir, entitled *Lost In Translation: Life in a New Language,* by the Polish-American writer Eva Hoffman. Feeling both betrayed and confused by what she describes as "this combination of rigid opinion and protean changeability" she found in America, she writes,

> There are no such things as fatal mistakes anymore, I say to my father in my mind, no irreversible choices, or irrevocable consequences. We live in a post-tragic condition. If you marry the wrong man, you can get divorced; if you start out on a wrong career, you can retrack and start another one; in this country, you can pick yourself up from bankruptcy, and a stint in jail; and you can always, of course, pick up stakes and head out, if not for another frontier, then at least for another town. There is no ultimate failure here, no undying shame—only new branchings, new beginnings, new game plans. Go to X; if that doesn't work, veer off to Y; and so on, and so on. That's what freedom is about, and we live in a free country, understand, Father?

"This is a society," Hoffman recalls a fellow student at Harvard telling her, "in which you are what you think you are. Nobody gives you your identity here, you have to reinvent yourself every day."

But to live out the American protean dream—as many Americans have and still do, either openly or "in the closet"—clearly also entails risks as well as liberties. Our essential proteanism, as Lifton points out, "imbues us with sometimes dangerous social and psychological vulnerabilities." We—or, on a more literal level, our resumés—can easily be dismissed as "unstable," "uncentered," "immature," "mercurial," "indecisive," and "unbalanced." For "America," as Hoffman writes,

> is the land of yearning, and perhaps no-
> where else are one's desires so wantonly
> stimulated; nowhere else is the compromise
> so difficult to achieve. Under the constant
> assaults of plenitude, it is difficult to agree
> to being just one person, and in order to
> achieve that simple identity, one may be
> driven to extreme paths.

Yet this yearning—this possibility of going to extremes—also provides Americans and our nation, no doubt, with part of our charm and allure, with the still-lingering *mythos* that America is the "land of opportunity," the "beacon of freedom," the last hope of many whose other hopes have been dimmed, or extinguished, by societies too rigid, too fixed, or too mired in their own past to accommodate the urgencies of ever-hungry, ever-changing selves, selves trying to find their way between the pre-determined rigidities of, say, rigid Marxist dogma and the perpetual dream of starting over that can place one forever, in the words of Jack Kerouac's famous title, *On The Road*.

In closing, then—because, as a poet and novelist who, in typical protean fashion, is merely "posing" as a scholar, it's my penchant to always want to close with a poem—let me do so with the closing lines of a poem entitled "Corson's Inlet," by the Pulitzer- and National Book Award-winning American poet, A. R. Ammons, lines which, I think, embody both the values of the proteanism and a certain essential truth about the American spirit, and which might be described as the "high" cultural equivalent of that famous "low" cultural 1970s bumper sticker bearing the words, *"Today is the first day of the rest of your life."* "I see narrow orders," Ammons declares at the end of his long free-verse poem,

WHEN HISTORY ENTERS THE HOUSE

limited tightness, but will
not run to that easy victory:
    still around the looser, wider forces work:
    I will try
to fasten into order enlarging gasps of disorder, widening
scope, but enjoying the freedom that
Scope eludes my grasp, that there is no finality of vision,
that I have perceived nothing completely,
    that tomorrow a new walk is a new walk.

April 1994

REPORT FROM
THE HOME FRONT

Just in case Hungarians are wondering what kinds of cultural and other surprises the triumph of capitalism might hold in store for them over the long run, here some of the news items that caught my attention during a recent month spent (as they say in the Foreign Service) "Stateside":

(1) In Kansas City, a booming new business (perhaps a sequel to New York Bagels here?), a bakery with a new twist by the name of *K. C. Canine*, has recently opened its doors, greeted by long lines of enthusiastic customers and their leashed appendages. The bakery, as you may have guessed from its name, offers a wide variety of baked goods (cookies, cakes, hot-dog shaped pastries, etc.), for the exclusive consumption of man's four-legged best friend. But, according to a report on National Public Radio, the delectable goods and their wafting aromas are apparently so seductive that a certain female shopper, not realizing it was a bakery for dogs, bought some dozen of the canine cookies and took them home to her husband (a man, I assume, not named "Spot"), who apparently so savored the luscious morsels that she returned the next day wanting to order an entire birthday cake! Buoyed

by its early success, according to NPR, *K.C. Canine* is considering expanding its repertoire...to include baked goods for cats.

(2) While we're on the subject of pets, a new lobbying group—complete with a small armada of well-paid lobbyists (all of them, no doubt, retired congressmen from the Louisiana Bayou or the Everglades) and an office in Washington, D. C.—has just been formed to protect the rights of yet another group unjustly overlooked in America's forward march toward cultural pluralism and equal representation. The National Herpetological Association, an organization invested with the sacred task of protecting the much-neglected equal rights of snake and reptile owners (for whose companions there are, for example, yet no bakeries), will shortly open its doors, with the hope of influencing and passing legislation that will assure that, henceforth, America's pluralistic democracy will not ignore the rights of those whose yearnings include, for example, the companionship of lizards and chameleons. Should you, on your next visit to your congressperson's office, spot an iguana or a boa constrictor slinking down the corridors of the Rayburn Building, don't worry: The humble creature is merely busy doing God's work on earth—standing up for his/her/its, and its owner's, equal rights.

(3) Think *you've* got money problems? Well, the National Baseball Players' Association, whose membership includes the youngest and most secure group of millionaires on the planet (*average* salary over $1.2 million annually (for six months' work), *minimum* a mere $150,000) has announced that its now-month-long strike will continue throughout the rest of the season, forcing—for the first time in its ninety-year history—the cancellation of America's time-honored spectacle, the World Series. The major issue involved in this strike by these much-aggrieved young athletes?? You guessed it: *more money.*

(4) The O. J. Simpson trial, which has filled the lacuna in the national attention caused by the cancellation of the rest of the baseball season, can now be seen live on *all* the major networks, including cable. Multi-million dollar book contracts, it is rumored, have already been signed by, or offered to, all the major attorneys and other players, both defense and prosecution, by—who else but those great guardians of American intellectual life?—the publishing companies.

(5) President Clinton, vacationing on Martha's Vineyard, has, according to detailed reports in all the major media, ridden a bike with his wife Hillary and daughter Chelsea; had dinner with authors William Styron, Gabriel Garcia Marquez and Carlos Fuentes; jammed on the saxophone with singer Carly Simon; read six "literary" books (a list of

the actual books purchased for the President at the local island bookstore was published by most of the major dailies); but, alas, seems still unable to realize his major ambition of breaking 80 on the golf course.

On a slightly more somber, but less interesting, note, it seems that the President's Health Care Program, which he promised would provide health insurance coverage "for every American," is irretrievably stalled amid partisan bickering in the Congress; but, yes, the President *will* deliver on his long-threatened promise to restore democracy by invading Haiti. The President, after all, in the great tradition of George Bush, is not a wimp.

In case none of the above, my fellow American expatriates, serves to cheer you concerning the ongoing life of your *alma mater,* I do have several pieces of good news with which to conclude: The water in Walden Pond is as clear and unpolluted as ever (if you just stay away from the Thoreau-seeking tourists on week-ends). It was a cool and intoxicatingly clear August in New England. There is—lest we fear that the gap between high and low culture is irretrievable—an interview with Madonna by (who else?) Norman Mailer in the current issue of *Esquire.* And if none of the above succeeds in moving you, there is always, for your intellectual diversion and amusement, the cover story on Oprah Winfrey's new, slightly less *bús*-y body, and new life, in *People* magazine.

It is, perhaps, yet another visitor to America, the Frenchman Alexis de Tocqueville, writing over a hundred years ago who, rather than I, should have the last word on all this:

> In democracies…all men are alike, and do things pretty nearly alike. It is true that they are subject to great and frequent vicissitudes; but as the same events of good or adverse fortune are continually recurring, the name of the actors only is changed, the piece is always the same. The aspect of American society is animated, because men and things are always changing; but it is monotonous, because all these changes are alike.

Egészségünkre és isten hozott …. Drink up. Welcome back.

SEPTEMBER 1994

"TRIUMPH OF THE TAWDRY": O. J. SIMPSON AND THE UNMAKING OF AMERICA

When Nobel Prize-winning Nigerian novelist Wole Soyinka, referring recently to the spread of American culture and the media's role in it, specifically singled out the O. J. Simpson circus as evidence of "the triumph of the tawdry," he was, in true writerly (as opposed to journalistic) fashion, engaging in the art of understatement. Brought to you by, essentially, the same coterie of the high-minded that gave us "Terminator," "Jurassic Park," "The Lion King"—and, lest we forget, that latest version of Eden, the Internet—the made-for-television Simpson affair (I won't, in this opening paragraph, dignify it by calling it a trial), garbed in the high rhetoric of justice and the public's much-touted "right to know," was, in fact, a kind of American apotheosis, the ultimate vision of democracy as doomsday.

The Simpson (okay, I'll say it) "trial" had everything (as has by now been pointed out so many times that only a writer doing hack-work would dare repeat it): sex, violence, race, money, celebrity, sports and even, for good measure, a tad of religion—everything, that is, that

197

America and its "New World Order" has by now become associated with. Occasionally referred to (I can only pray, with a touch of irony) as "America's 'King Lear,'" it left little doubt as to which of the three words in that sacrilegious title deserved to be highlighted: The Simpson trial, in large measure *was* contemporary America—a massive civic education program in greed, vanity, decadence, injustice, and trivia, as triumphant in its tawdriness as any event in the recollection of modern memory.

For, above all, it might be said that the significance of the Simpson trial, exactly paralleled by the rise in the significance of wealth and celebrity themselves, lies in its utter reversal of all once-time-honored measures of significance: Before you could mouth the letters "O. J.," in fact, the case's most salient fact—the two brutally murdered young people and their decimated families—was lost in a flurry of high-priced lawyers, publicity-famished witnesses, journalistic graphomania, and racially incited rhetoric so high-pitched and ubiquitous that it required the occasional grieving outbursts of *la famille Goldman*, sandwiched as they were between hoards of scribbling journalists, to remind us that anyone was dead to begin with.

"The ceremony of innocence is drowned," wrote the ever-prescient Yeats in "The Second Coming," and here too—beneath the always inscrutable and gorgeously light brown, multi-million-dollar face of soon-to-be-even-richer Orenthal James Simpson—the innocent dead and the innocent grieving were drowned out. In fact, as the so-called "race card" (it was not, in fact, a card, but a blotter), so clearly present from the very outset, began to be played less and less subtly as the trial reached its utterly believable *dénouement*—the English language itself, rather than mere justice, increasingly seemed under attack, with words like "facts," "reasonable," and "doubt," to mention only a few, quickly relegated to some futuristic linguistic netherworld in which meaning no longer will *mean* at all. ("The future," as the famous American bumpersticker goes, "is now.")

"Why be an American," a friend of mine once asked rhetorically, "if you can't take a joke?" And there was much in the Simpson trial that— if it weren't, on deeper reflection, so ominous and sad—should have catapulted even the most lugubrious of spirits into paroxysms of laughter. How, for example, was it humanly possible that a man as ferociously determined to escape from the Black world as was O. J. Simpson—complete with his beautiful blond wife (and girlfriends), his house in one of Los Angeles' most exclusive white communities, his Nixon- and Bush-like golf games at all-white country clubs, and his disavowal of Black causes so glaring it made Pat Robertson look like Martin Luther King—could become, overnight, a symbol of racial injustice and Black oppression? Rodney King, perhaps; maybe even Mike Tyson. But Orenthal James Simpson? The thought, quite simply, boggles the mind.

On one level, of course, the Simpson case *was*, indeed, a triumph of racial equality. For Simpson, along with convicted rapist Tyson and his twice-convicted (of murder) boxing promoter Don King, can now safely take their place among the gallery of whites such as Watergate burglar-turned-novelist John Erlichman, convicted former Vice President Spiro Agnew, and Los Angeles whoremistress-to-the-stars Heidi Fleiss (whose memoirs, no doubt, will shortly be published) in affirming the American-as-apple-pie theory that crime not only pays, and pays big, but it is as color-blind as our (amended) Constitution…with liberty and money for all.

Indeed, anyone with even a badly malfunctioning irony detector will have no trouble whatsoever finding gold in the veins of the Simpson media mine: The sight, to give merely one more example, of the one Black man utterly reduced to tears by the verdict—not, of course, Simpson himself (whose winning and slightly demonic smirk exposed not the vindicated relief of an unjustly accused innocent, but the cynical contempt of one who, using its own weapons against it, had beaten the system)—but, of all people, the dignified and trapped (by his own nation's racial politics and stereotypes) Black prosecutor, Christopher Darden. The sight of Darden, overcome with tears and unable to continue speaking at the post-verdict prosecution press conference, became, to my mind, a metaphor for the travesty of justice, the perverse inversion of racial projections and counter-projections, into which the Simpson trial descended. Odd as it may seem, it was in the figure of Darden—sad, melancholic, grieving, betrayed—much more than of Simpson himself, that it might be said that the pathos and humiliation of *l'affaire Simpson* was incarnated.

But perhaps the saddest revelation exposed by the Simpson trial, of course, is the fact that insofar as individual human beings are concerned, they are, in the eyes of the media and general public, vestigial creatures, replaced by beings whose only human function is to act as emblazoned "stand-ins" for stereotypes and clichés—to wit, the sexy and sex-starved blond who lusts after Black men (Nicole); the sexually potent and athletically adept, nearly white, and white-woman-hungry Black (Simpson); the innocent Jewish victim (Goldman); the tough-as-nails white professional woman (Clark); the slick-and-savvy, Black, race-is-everything advocate (Cochran); the liberal Jewish lawyer (Shapiro); the loud-mouthed, compensatorily intellectual Jewish nerd (Dershowitz); the bigoted white cop (Fuhrman), and the sensitively melancholic, though rage-filled, Black man (Darden), to name but a few.

In fact, another thing the Simpson trial might be said to "stand for" (if, indeed, it "stands for" anything) is that all of America has now become one big, happy, affirmative-actioned family in which everyone stands for something and no one, heaven forbid, stands for him- or herself. So hungry for meaning do we seem to be in our increasingly meaningless (and, not accidentally, media-filled) lives that, like a lonely and self-hating man looking for love, we find it everywhere except in the place we should most be seeking it...ourselves.

Perhaps now, as I near the end of this piece, the time may be ripe for a small confession. I was not, throughout this long and seeemingly relentless media circus, much interested in it, and expended (it seemed to me) much more energy in its avoidance (no small effort) than its pursuit. But on the evening on which the verdict was finally handed down by the jury, I found myself in a kind of moral dilemma all my own: Whether to attend evening Kol Nidre services to mark the beginning of the holiest day of the Jewish year, Yom Kippur, the Day of Atonement, or to stay home and watch the verdict delivered. Perhaps it was the infidel in me, or the writer, or the cynic—or all three—but I must confess, dear Lord, that I chose the latter.

Nonetheless, for this Jew, at least—and for the family of the murdered Ronald Goldman, I'm certain—the evening came full circle as I watched the crowd outside the Los Angeles County Courthouse erupt in jubilation, and Mrs. Goldman erupt in tears, as the verdict was read. It occurred to me that, like it or not, the evening was still, at its very core, somehow concerned with atonement, and with an inscrutable God who, at that very moment, must have been scribbling inscrutable verdicts in his good Book of Life and Death.

It also occurred to me as I listened to those roars of jubilation outside the Los Angeles County Courtroom that, just as it is said, in a democracy, that a people get the government they deserve, they get the heroes they deserve as well. And—as those cheers went up, who could deny it? At this particular moment in American—and perhaps, alas, the world's—history: *"O. J., he's our man."* Just ask *Time.*

Shortly after the verdict was announced—by a jury one of whose members left the courtroom brandishing the clenched-fist Black Power salute, lest we forget what it was really about—Simpson let it be known that he would now devote much of his long pent-up energies to a search for "the real killer(s)." In that sense, too, he's a lucky man. He won't have far to look. Any mirror will do.

October 1995

REAL FAMILY VALUES

It is a kind of psychological truism that, the more frequently one tends to discuss a subject (sex, travel and love being the three conspicuous examples), the less one is likely to be any good at it. ("'Twere profanation of our joys," the wise poet John Donne so eloquently put it, "to tell the laity our love.") Many of us, I suspect, have had the experience of the prospective lover who, orgasmic over cocktails, is a Valium in the sack. Or the would-be Hemingway who, while turning in a hypothalmic haste to the Travel Section of the Sunday *New York Times,* remains safely sequestered all his adult days in the quasi-urban condom of Duluth.

Family values, that beeline of meal tickets to the great sentimental heart of the American electorate, has, particularly as the American election season looms, no lack of verbal cheerleaders as well—most of whom, rest assured, do everything within their unfamilial power to stay as far removed from any real contact with family (or, for that matter, values) as they can. When, for example, has anyone last seen Newt Gingrich, that great divorcer of post-operative spouses and guardian of our collective futures, even remotely within germ-range of a five-year-old—aside, that is, from when he is being followed by a photographer from *The Washington Post.* Or, to be non-partisan about the matter, can you possibly imagine Warren Christopher risking a drool-stain on his new suit?

The same folks who are all hot for family values are, of course, tumescent for trickle-down capitalism as well (the two being not-very-distant cousins), so you can bet your *csizma*s that—if any of them have ever stopped in Hungary for *goulash* with the late József Antall or a *lángos* with Lajos Bokros or Gyula Horn—they haven't made a week-end stop at the *Bábszínház* Puppet Theater on Andrássy út as well. After all, a cultural experience for children of the very highest artistic and imaginative quality that can be had for a mere 200 *forints* can't, in the greater scheme of things that trickle, really seep down very far...or can it?

The existence of high-quality, low-cost culture (I won't degrade it by referring to it as "entertainment") for children in Central/Eastern Europe (those poor, deprived Communist backwaters we Americans so loved to hate), of course, far predates the Brave New World of 1989. In fact—and one needn't be a vestigial 'lefty' to concede this—it was precisely the lack of a profit motive (and the obvious *un*profitability of devoting such labor-intensive care to such capital-discouraging low prices) that made these kinds of cultural institutions for children—brought to you *not* by Procter & Gamble, but by the State—possible. Not merely those institutions, I might add, but also first-class, affordable day care, a vast array of beautiful and well-maintained public playgrounds, and a general public who—essentially mute to the rhetoric of "family values" and "securing our children's future"—seems to genuinely *love* children...and not just their own.

Sitting at the puppet theatre this morning with my son (an experience which, in all honesty, I don't personally adore, but adore watching *him* adore), I couldn't help but think that—just as a reading of Tocqueville's *Democracy in America* or *Huckleberry Finn* should be required reading for anyone wishing to understand our strangely democratic America, a visit to the *Bábszínház* at 69 Andrássy út (now, before it's too late, and some budding Hungarian-American entrepreneur from New Jersey discovers it and turns it into a Burger King) might be a prerequisite for understanding socialism—and why so many of its now-dispossessed citizens are pulling the levers for yet another dose of it—as well. For, insofar as the world of children and their actual well-being is concerned, my years here among the still-penumbral "socialist" institutions of Central/Eastern Europe have convinced me that there exists, in the vernacular of free enterprise, a tremendous confusion between profiting *from* and profiting *by*. "For what is a man profited," the *Bábszínház* seems to ask, along with (no pun intended) the prophet Matthew, "if he shall gain the whole world, and lose his own soul?" "No profit grows," my son's smiling face testifies along with Shakespeare, "where is no pleasure ta'en."

Now, admittedly, if like Gingrich & Co. you've got your sights set on *big* goals—like the abolition of the National Endowments for the Arts and Humanities, for example, or the defeat of National Health Care—I can't imagine there's much solace, or diversion, in store for you by sitting through a Saturday morning performance of *Misi Mókus*, or attending a Sunday afternoon cocoa concert for children at the Merlin Theatre with Iván Fischer and members of the Budapest Festival Orchestra...all for little more than the price of a Coke. I can't imagine, for that matter, that, next time you're in town, you'd care to visit my son's $20-a-month *óvoda,* or go for a ride through the beautiful Buda hills on the socialist-founded Children's Railway for less than a buck. Why, after all, waste your time on such inanities when—for about $150 for a family of four—you can spend a decibel-filled day at Disney World and give the Dow Jones a kick in the pants to boot?

"We are the world," sings Michael Jackson, whose experiences with the occupants of the second half of his refrain, some suspect, have been relatively licentious, "we are the children." But, at such prices, alas, it's a world only a few children, and their struggling, two-career parents, can afford. No, my fellow Americans, after all, we're a busy, profit-motivated people. There are important things to be dealt with and discussed: flat taxes, the Contract with America, sex, love, travel...and, of course, let's not forget: *family values.*

DECEMBER 1995

SIGHT FOR SORE HEARTS

A book goes a long way. Overkill in cultural matters is not an optional strategy, it is a necessity, since selective cultural targeting spells defeat no matter how well one's aim is taken.

JOSEPH BRODSKY, *An Immodest Proposal*

I walk into what was, until recently, the American Library in Budapest and the three of them are listlessly seated there, a bit like three members of a now-extinct species resurrected in a world they can no longer comprehend. These three women—Ildikó, Ági and Éva—once guardians of the American cultural and literary presence in this great city, are about to become guardians of a very different kind of presence, a "high-tech business resource center" whose substitution for that library, in the hearts and coffers of the nation of which I am a citizen, represents a dismal metaphor for America's present cultural condition.

207

WHEN HISTORY ENTERS THE HOUSE

Yes, the holdings of the American Library in Budapest will no doubt find, or have already found, an alternative sponsor and home. [Ed.'s note: The library was transfered to ELTE University in early 1997.] But the handing over of this already minimal cultural commitment from public to private hands, represents—on a deeper, metaphorical level— a shift in America's cultural and financial priorities that should be a cause of alarm to all of its citizens, at home *or* abroad. Our first and only East European-born American Poet Laureate, the late Joseph Brodsky—who, in the above-cited address at the Library of Congress in 1991, proposed a government-subsidized printing of *fifty million* copies of an anthology of American poetry priced at two dollars a copy—must surely be turning over in his freshly dug grave at the thought.

Even prior to the closing of the American Library, the American cultural presence in a city such as Budapest—as compared, say, to that of France or Germany—was a paltry thing, so far inferior to America's support for, and visibility in, the business community that it in itself testified to the devalued priority America places on its own culture. Nonetheless, the library was the one institution in Budapest which provided both to American expatriates and, more importantly, Hungarians of all ages, free and readily available access to those treasures of American literature and culture which made our nation a model for freedom of expression for much of the civilized world. Not only my students, but schoolchildren and adults of all ages, Hungarian writers, colleagues and friends, our Hungarian neighbors, and members of the international community in general, looked to that place—sponsored and supported by *our* government—as the one reliable resource with which to satisfy their innate curiosity about America and its culture.

Indeed, it is still, the irrefutable evidence notwithstanding, utterly unimaginable to me that there exists even a single American taxpayer who—having seen, as I saw daily, a young Hungarian boy or girl turning the pages of Walt Whitman's *Leaves of Grass* or Emily Dickinson's *Collected Poems* or *The Collected Speeches of Abraham Lincoln* in the library's reading room—could possibly maintain that such a facility was not one of the wisest, and most precious, investments of American dollars abroad, *particularly* in a time of world-wide economic crisis and belt-tightening.

Defending the library's closing on the grounds that "the need is greatest for a high-tech resource center," a member of the USIA staff here in Budapest commented several months ago that since "now you can get *Time* magazine on newsstands, the days of need for that [the library]

208

are over." But it is precisely *because* of the danger that *Time* magazine may be equated with American culture—that *Dallas* may be taken for *Moby Dick*, John Grisham for Ralph Ellison, William Safire for H. L. Mencken—that the need for such a facility as the American Library, rather than for yet another "high-tech resource center," is most urgent.

For what makes me—and, I think, most thinking Americans—proudest of our country and its heritage are *not* its Bill Gateses and Donald Trumps and Ross Perots (though they surely serve their purpose) but rather its Hemingways and Dickinsons and Lincolns and Jeffersons and Ellisons and Bishops and Morrisons and Bellows...names which, if not for the presence of such places as the American Library, may slowly become unknown outside our own borders.

Wallace Stevens, the great American businessman/poet famous for his many notable aphorisms concerning American life and the role of poetry in it, observed that "money is a kind of poetry"—a kind of poetry, we might note, that America has done more than its share to distribute around the world. But Stevens also said—on the subject of *real* poetry, and, implicitly, of real culture in general—that its purpose was "to help us live our lives"...something no "high-tech resource center," and no amount of purely private money, can do.

It seemed to me—as I left, no doubt for the last time, the once publicly funded American Library in Budapest—that the saddened expressions I saw on the faces of my three Hungarian-born librarian friends were trying to tell me something. It was, I suspect, something not only about them, but about us—and about the dangerous direction in which our once-proud country is headed in these troubled, soul-tightening times.

April 1996

HOMESICK AT LAST

It begins as a dull ache in the pit of the stomach, a nagging absence of something, an ellipse that suddenly stutters about in the soul, making you feel like a walking suture with legs, a something missing, a wound. Perhaps it begins as a diminution in your appetite for the new, a suddenly lagging sense of wonder at what were once the novelties surrounding you, an increasing impatience at the foreign post office, a growing irritability at your inability to master anything more than the now-tedious small-talk of *"jó reggelt"* and *"köszönöm szépen"* and *"hol tanulsz beszélni angolul?"*

Somehow, being congratulated on your pronunciation of *viszontlátásra* no longer suffices to build up your self-esteem: Your soul could use a Geritol-shake of reinforcement in your native vernacular. You are already much less charming (or, for that matter, cheerful) even in your own tongue (which, horror of horrors, you realize YOU are beginning to speak with a foreign accent!) than you once were, and, in someone else's, you're quite simply: a disaster. Places you once would never even have considered dropping in on—bars full of loud, boisterous, drunken Australian rugby types and IRA veterans (no place for a nice

Jewish boy like you) now cry out to you in the passionate, arousing syllables of a lost lover. You'd prefer, in fact, a moronic conversation with a barbell salesman in your own language to lunch with a Nobel Prize-winner in theirs. (Milan Kundera or Mike Tyson? I'll take Iron Mike, thank you.)

It's quite enough, by now, having your French wife talk about "the *statue quo*" and "deviating" the conversation without having to struggle—a shit-eating, phony half-smile crawling moronically onto your face—to mouth the inexpressible phrase, *"Annyira vágytam rád az éjszaka, hogy nem tudtam aludni"* ("I desired you so much during the night, that I couldn't sleep") to the eighteen-year-old Hungarian girl in see-through white tights who hands you a lard-soaked piece of baked dough known as a *pogácsa* in the 24-hour *csemege*. Why not just head for your once-neighborhood Dunkin' Donuts and grab a Boston creme and a large coffee-to-go from the undergraduate accounting major at Salem State who, at least, tells you to "Have a nice day" in a tongue you can make sense of?

"I liked being alone with English," frumpy, competitive Gertrude is rumored to have said. And if that's how she liked it, that's, no doubt, what she deserved to be: alone. (Or, worse yet, alone with no one but *ersatz*-macho Hemingway and douty old Alice.) We all, eventually, wind up with the face we deserve, and the company as well. Thought you'd never *ever* in your life miss Bryant Gumbel? Homesick for Camille Paglia, or female students who go running to the Dean and charge you with attempted sodomy for brushing against their overcoats? Well, try stuttering around in Budapest for a couple of years in cracked *Magyar* and see if you wouldn't pay your last damned deflated *forint* for breakfast with Connie Chung.

Never much of a socializer to begin with, grouch and curmudgeon that you always were, did you ever think the day would come when you would heed the Biblical indictment to "love thy neighbor as thyself"? But what wouldn't you give, these days, to gaze into the mirror and see, staring back, the pimply diabetic who once played Ultimate Spinach albums full-tilt at 3:00 a.m. in the apartment next to yours?

Nasty and competitive in a former life, dismissive of your colleagues, crass and mean-spirited behind the backs of your rivals, how your once mean-spirited little heart aches, now, for someone you hated shouting a *Hi-yo Silver away!* at you in perfect English. (Even an, "Eat it, you lousy little kike!," you realize, would be welcome.) Martin Amis, that divinely talented little upper-class prick who hardly ever leaves gossipy little England, says writers *ought* to hate each other, but how much time has *he* ever spent, you wonder, trying to explain to an emergency room physician in Hungarian that his wife, *a la* Irena Bobbitt, has just zipped his schlong into his suit pants while letting out the waistband?

"So sure of victory at last is the courage that can wait," said Mark Twain, but what if you're no longer very courageous about your foreignness and—like a two-year-old having to make ka-ka on the "A" train—can't wait very much longer to get the hell home, the place where, when you say, "Hey, buddy, can I borrow a dime?" nobody answers, *"Sajnos, mester, nem beszélek angolul."* All roads, a wise man once told me (in English), finally lead to humility...so why shouldn't this one? Weren't sixteen years in a family whose parents, though leeward of Ellis Island, kept putting *umlauts* over their *o*'s more than enough? Why, now, spend sixteen more in a country where one kind of *umlaut* isn't even enough, and they've invented a long (*ő*) and a short (*ö*) one just to make sure you never, *ever* get to have a real conversation in this crazy, unlearnable tongue?

Even the New York Bagels across the street, which you once viewed (rightfully) as a symptom of the triumph of the cheap and homogenized over all forms of cultural difference, now calls out to you, not merely for the taste and texture of its soft, chewy, New York-reminiscent dough, but for the sheer beauty of its bi-syllabic name: *B-A-G-E-L*, your tongue gliding over each precious letter, spelling it out as you pass, a sight and sound which, in your now-homesick heart, no lardy *lángos* will ever again be able to compare with.

When you first arrived, thrilled with the freedom of having "escaped" (escaped from *what?*, you now wonder), it was Endre Ady and József Attila you mostly heeded, but now, with a lump the size of an NBA basketball in your throat, it's Hawthorne: "Amid the seeming confusion of our mysterious world," ends the great *American* master's bone-chilling short story, "Wakefield*," "individuals are so nicely adjusted to a system, and systems to one another, and to a whole, that, by stepping aside for a moment, *A MAN EXPOSES HIMSELF TO A FEARFUL RISK OF LOSING HIS PLACE FOREVER."* And now you wonder as you sit here typing on the fifth floor of 19/B Bajcsy-Zsillinszky út, dread creeping all over your middle-aged body like a child's chickenpox, if you, silly fool, have also lost your place forever.

"I am homesick always," ends a poem whose author and title I can't for the moment (being too homesick myself) remember, and maybe we are. But why make it worse for yourself in a country and language you feel, ultimately (and you're getting very close to the ultimately) and utterly deracinated in, without recourse to the smart, savvy, funny, English-speaking self you for so long, and so arduously, nurtured and cultivated?

"Sorry to hear you're in exile. Whatever for?" wrote your friend the poet, wiser and happier than you in his New York apartment. "I didn't think anything short of plagiarism could exile a poet; no one knows we're on the map in the first place.... Four years sounds like an eternity to be that far from home."

It is. And suddenly, as you write this, you realize that, finally, yet another kind of history has entered the house: your own.

MAY 1996

WHAT I LOVETH WELL
REMAINS AMERICAN

Boise. Idaho. I've been "out West" here before. Almost exactly twenty years ago—in October of 1976 to be precise—at the invitation of the late poet Richard Hugo, I quit my job in Washington, D. C., sold all the belongings that wouldn't fit into my used Toyota station wagon, broke up with my girlfriend, and moved to Missoula, Montana.

It was a classic case, alas often repeated in my later life, of the wrong act at the wrong time: After nearly a month in a (pink, to my recollection) hovel euphemistically called The Sweet Rest Motel and a single night in a newly rented apartment, I woke, stuffed my just-unpacked belongings back into my wagon, fastened my seatbelt, and, as they say in the West, "hightailed it" back East just as fast as my panic-stricken-compressed gas pedal could get me there. Within a month, I was working at Time-Life Books in Alexandria, Virginia, safely ensconced once again in a world of less sky and more concrete...a world where Europe, at least, was only an ocean away.

When people those days asked me why I fled Montana in such a panic, I had a rather glib, but not-untruthful, response: "Too American," I'd say, in only a slight variation of a phrase a friend of mine had once used to explain his flight from the suburbs: "Too many trees." The West, or what I saw and sensed of it at the time, *was* too "American" for me, too filled, that is, with certain idiosyncrasies and intonations that perhaps only America, in all the world, properly owns. Nowhere else, for example, had I ever observed such a seeming disproportion of sky to earth, of nature to humanity, of wildlife to human life. Nowhere else had I ever walked into a bar where the main topic of conversation was how to find sufficient freezer space for your freshly slaughtered elk. Nowhere else had I ever encountered grandmothers and grandfathers who didn't speak with a German, Yiddish, or at least an Italian, accent. Nowhere else had I ever said "thank you" to people and had them answer, "You bet."

The West—particularly the "wild" West of places like Montana and Idaho—terrified me back in 1976 partly because, as I put it at the time, "it isn't on the way to anywhere"...a kind of second-generation euphemism for saying that it wasn't on the way to New York or Europe. America, in my immigrant-oriented eyes, was not so much America as an ocean-crossed extension of Europe, a place where you weren't "American," but merely a Greek, Italian, Polish, Hispanic or Chinese living on borrowed turf. America was a place where you could take a walk in "nature"—i. e., an urban park—and still come out on the other side to find a bagel and a cappuccino. America was a place where a night crawler was an infant who had escaped from his crib.

Having spent the last four years in Central Europe, being married to a French wife, and now living, at least temporarily, in the Middle East, I've found that, for expatriates, America-bashing can become a kind of recreational activity ("re-creating," in the process, a sense of home), a way both of justifying your choices and reminding yourself, in a playful and not-too-disturbing way, of the country and culture which—despite anything and all you may do to have it otherwise—are yours. Part of the pride and pleasure of being an American, after all, is that there's so much to make fun of. (America, let's not forget, is the nation that has made comic self-mockery into an art form...and excessive love of country into a right-wing threat.)

"You loved them well and they remain," the poet Hugo wrote of the people in his small town, "still with nothing to do, no money and no will." And now, as I contemplate Hugo and Montana and Europe and Boise, it occurs to me that one of my own human failings may have been that—with all their human flaws, comedies and foibles—I haven't loved my fellow Americans well enough. Twenty years, three continents, and two marriages later, I realize that what I may have been partly fleeing from when I took off in a purple haze from Missoula was a certain deeply rooted, though submerged, *Americaness* within myself.

Driving my rented car up Idaho Highway 21 out of Boise past—where else could you find such a name?—Lucky Peak, and toward the old Gold Rush town of Idaho City the other night, I found myself marveling at all that beautiful sky, the parched but massive Ponderosa pines yearning for rain. I stopped the car just to pause and inhale, and the air was so clean and still I swear I heard the sound of some distant fisherman's fly touching down on a stream. There wasn't a bagel or a cappuccino for miles, but I kept turning my head in all directions, hoping to spot an elk. If I stopped at the little 24-hour grocery in the shack around the bend, I could be dead certain the person inside would speak English, the one language (all dilettanteries aside) I know well enough to truly love.

Tonight, when I turn over early in my rented motel room to sleep, the frenzied crowd in the football stadium across the road, screaming their lungs out on behalf of a team called the Broncos, will most likely keep me awake. There's sky all around me, and the closest thing to an accent I've heard thus far the distinction between upcountry and down. Thus far at least, though I've only been here a week, no one's asked me to stay. But, if they do, the odds are better than even money that, pausing for a moment to clear the other languages and international cobwebs from my too-long-exiled psyche, I'll turn for a moment, look up at the sky, and answer, "You bet."

SEPTEMBER 1996

Public bath, Budapest. (Photo by Susan Kaufman.)

EPILOGUE

Lukács Fürdő

DECEMBER 31, 1995

Why should I not be among them?—
the old man with the face of an angelfish
whose balls sag like overripe apricots
as he glides; the lamed *nagymama*s,
their double chins bellowing out
like frill-necked lizards; the aging professors
still revising their footnotes as they swim;
and the old seamstress, her left hand
taking on a life of its own as she strokes,
parting the waters like an injured eel?

Why should I not be among them?—
the old Jewish writers whose pens have run dry,
and the squidish satyrs, their ink gone too,
this floating democracy of back pain and arthritis, flesh-
bedecked former sybarites
who tread and stroke, who will gather,
later, in the sauna like a *Kaffee-Klatsch*
of cardless bridge players,
where I will relish the grim satisfaction
of being the youngest among them,
a man who, not wanting to resemble
his father, resembles his grandmother.

So why should I not be here?—
anticipating my own destiny,
ontogeny recapitulating phylogeny
as we glide, on impaired limbs
(scrinching our balls back
into their scrotums) downward
to darkness, hoping to rectify
these god-given bodies, cleansing
ourselves of earthly pain, trying
to heal ourselves before we are healed.

219

Books from Pleasure Boat Studio

William Slaughter, THE POLITICS OF MY HEART
(ISBN 0-9651413-0-6)

Frances Driscoll, THE RAPE POEMS
(ISBN 0-9651413-1-4)

Michael Blumenthal, WHEN HISTORY ENTERS THE HOUSE:
ESSAYS FROM CENTRAL EUROPE
(ISBN 0-9651413-2-2)

Tung Nien, SETTING OUT: THE EDUCATION OF LI-LI
Translated by Mike O'Connor
(ISBN 0-9651413-3-0)

From *Pleasure Boat Studio,*
an essay written by Ouyang Xiu,
Song Dynasty poet, essayist, and scholar,
on the twelfth day of the twelfth month
in the *renwu* year (January 25, 1043)

I have heard of men of antiquity who fled from the world to distant rivers and lakes and refused to their dying day to return. They must have found some source of pleasure there. If one is not anxious for profit, even at the risk of danger, or is not convicted of a crime and forced to embark; rather, if one has a favorable breeze and gentle seas and is able to rest comfortably on a pillow and mat, sailing several hundred miles in a single day, then is boat travel not enjoyable? Of course, I have no time for such diversions. But since 'pleasure boat' is the designation of boats used for such pastimes, I have now adopted it as the name of my studio. Is there anything wrong with that?

THE LITERARY WORKS OF OU-YANG HSIU
Translated by Ronald Egan
Cambridge University Press
New York, 1984